'A timely book in the current soci[...]
collection of contemporary and a[...]
literacy. It explores real life and w[...]
people can identify with. It nurtu[...]
to arm against the damaging im[...]
everyday racism.'

– *Kwame Opoku, National Black Police Association*

'While we have made some progress around how we attend to everyday discriminations, we also need timely reminders that there is still much to do. Cousins, in this superb text, offers challenge in a powerful but accessible way; not an easy task. This is a highly recommended work that should be read not only because of its own merit, but because it really makes us think.'

– *Dr Andrew Reeves, Associate Professor in the Counselling Professions and Mental Health and Chair of BACP*

'Susan Cousins offers a fresh approach to thinking about racism. For BAME readers it's a vital self-realisation approach which offers ways to explore identity and focus on wellbeing in order to thrive despite experiencing racism every day. It has reached into my heart as a white woman, helped me accept my privilege and recognise my clumsy attempts at understanding. Exquisitely written and simply brilliant.'

– *Professor Karen Holford, Deputy Vice-Chancellor, Cardiff University*

'I welcome this powerfully, insightful, thought provoking handbook. Long overdue and timely. From self-acceptance to purpose in life are the fundamental tools we need to remain strong and proud!'

- *Suzanne Duval BEM, BME Mental Health Manager, Diverse Cymru*

'Susan Cousins' *Overcoming Everyday Racism* is simultaneously both wonderfully relatable and greatly thought-provoking. Cousins' account of the experiences of many people of colour manages to perfectly highlight the issues that are prevalent in our society. I found it thoroughly enjoyable and well worth the read.'

– Hélèna Corcoran, LLM Student, University of Nottingham

'This is a timely book revisiting race and identity as we face a time of division and uncertainty. This book should provoke greater discussion and insight into who we are and what kind of country we want to live in.'

– Vaughan Gething Assembly Member for
Cardiff South and Penarth

OVERCOMING EVERYDAY RACISM

of related interest

How to Understand Your Gender
A Practical Guide for Exploring Who You Are
Alex Iantaffi and Meg-John Barker
Foreword by S. Bear Bergman
ISBN 978 1 78592 746 1
eISBN 978 1 78450 517 2

White Privilege Unmasked
How to Be Part of the Solution
Judy Ryde
ISBN 978 1 78592 408 8
eISBN 978 1 78450 767 1

Anxiety is Really Strange
Steve Haines
Illustrated by Sophie Standing
ISBN 978 1 84819 389 5 (paperback)
ISBN 978 1 84819 407 6 (hardback)
eISBN 978 0 85701 345 3

OVERCOMING EVERYDAY RACISM

Building Resilience and Wellbeing
in the Face of Discrimination
and Microagressions

SUSAN COUSINS Snr Acred MBACP
with CHERYL HILL, MRCOT

Jessica Kingsley *Publishers*
London and Philadelphia

Figure 2.2 adapted from the Wheel of Life© concept developed by Paul J. Meyer. Copyright © The Meyer Resource Group, Inc. ALL RIGHTS RESERVED

First published in 2019
by Jessica Kingsley Publishers
73 Collier Street
London N1 9BE, UK
and
400 Market Street, Suite 400
Philadelphia, PA 19106, USA

www.jkp.com

Copyright © Susan Cousins 2019

Library of Congress Cataloging in Publication Data
A CIP catalog record for this book is available from the Library of Congress

British Library Cataloguing in Publication Data
A CIP catalogue record for this book is available from the British Library

ISBN 978 1 78592 850 5
eISBN 978 1 78592 851 2

Printed and bound in Great Britain

To Tod and Alex, the very best of me.

In memory of my brother John-Paul, gone too soon.

For my Mother and Father, wherever they may be.

Acknowledgements

A very special thank you to Sara Nowakowski for reading the manuscript and providing feedback and suggestions. The writing of this book was made possible by the generous support of Cheryl Hill whose motivation proved invaluable Thank you to Sarah Hamlin for her perseverance and belief and to Emily Badger, Emma Holak and Karina Maduro at Jessica Kingsley Publishers. Many thanks to family and friends who have brought much support, fun, commitment and encouragement to this journey.

Contents

Introduction

This book arose out of my experience of living in a white majority culture and from facing the everyday complications of a life lived as a visible minority. The struggle to find an identity that sits well with me and that allows me to feel comfortable in my own skin has been a lifelong effort. There were many barriers that thwarted my desire to define myself, but eventually I discovered an identity that suited me, belonged to me, and at last I feel at home. However, I do intend to 'move house'. I do not have a single identity and I cannot put into words who I am and who I have or will become. What I do know is that my humanity is now no longer rooted in how not to offend white people.

I do not believe in pushing my viewpoint over and above yours. I'm hoping this book will allow you to explore and develop tools to find your own way, making choices that suit you and support you in navigating your world in your direction of flow.

The American Civil Rights Movement of the 1950s and 1960s has provided us with an inspirational legacy. Those who took part in the struggle for social justice are deserving of a huge amount of gratitude as the Movement is still very much alive in our current thinking and still contributing to current debate.

The American Civil Rights Movement gave birth to writers such as Angela Davis, James Baldwin, Toni Morrison and Langston Hughes to name but a few. And yet in the last couple of years, new narratives have emerged, narratives distinctly born out of a UK experience. Books such as *Slay In Your Lane: The Black Girl Bible*

(Adegoke and Uviebiné 2018), *The Good Immigrant* (Shukla 2016), *Why I'm No Longer Talking to White People About Race* (Eddo-Lodge 2017) and *Brit(ish): On Race, Identity and Belonging* (Hirsch 2018) all speak with new and distinct British voices. Books played a role then and now in influencing how we understand modern everyday racism and its continuous mutations. This new generation of literature is like a breath of fresh air, filling our lungs with a brand-new mood – a mood you felt but couldn't explain, but now it has been written down, Black, Asian and Minority Ethnic (BAME) people across the country are beginning to feel and think that at last their voices are out there living and breathing out new spaces. And they are powerful antidotes to lazy thinking, stereotypes and the generalisations we are all prey to.

When other people inflicted their definitions of my identity on me I found this problematic. As a young person, I became defensive and even justifiably angry because there was no support and no help within the education system at that time that offered any understanding in relation to the lived experience of exclusion because of the colour of my skin.

I had no idea that this positioning and imposing were about others feeling threatened – so threatened that they were not interested in asking me who I was but were insistent on their own imaginings and concepts surrounding my identity – enabling their safety and their sense of belonging within society. Enabling them to feel at home.

I grew up surrounded by the notion of black as a political term in a particular moment in history. My racial background has never been and still is not easily definable and I am often thought of as African Caribbean, South American and Asian. My sense of identity was complicated by my adoption into a multi-racial family and this led me to want certainty and choice about my identity. I could not relate to the word 'brown', I preferred the political 'black', and I fall in and out of describing myself as Indian and black. My origins are most likely to be from Southern India, but having been abandoned on the pavements of Mumbai and picked up by the police to spend months in an orphanage has left me bereft of any certainty. A sense of stability came in the form of my relationship to the struggles that were taking place in the United States and my involvement in the anti-apartheid movement in the UK during the 1980s. The personal struggles I endured on the streets where I was subjected to many forms of verbal and physical abuse served to shore up an even stronger sense of who I was and who I still am.

I was greatly influenced by notions of 'blackness' that were coming out of the Civil Rights Movement in the 60s. I wanted to direct my energies into the cause of social justice, connect with black people both in the States and in South Africa. I wanted to use the word 'black' because the categorisation connected me with the struggles in other parts of the world that echoed my own encounters with prejudice and discrimination. I would try and explain that I was using the term 'black' as a political naming of myself but this mostly fell on deaf or defensive ears. And once again I was defined by others who held more power than me.

Being raised in a family of seven brothers and sisters, all of whom were the consequence of transracial and transnational inter-country adoptions, was and still is an unusual and unique experience that left me confused and unsure of my own identity. We ought to have control over how we define ourselves, even if we get this wrong at times. It is our journey and one that is also unique. We should not feel compelled to take within ourselves others' definitions, feelings, thoughts and perceptions of who we are. I only did so to make others feel at ease with me and to 'fit in' to a society that felt unwelcoming. I absorbed their baggage as if it were my own to carry at great cost to myself. If you know yourself, it is easier to make sense of the world and make choices that are self-directed and not hand-me-downs from a bygone era.

I was 9 years old when I was asked to dress up as an Indian doll and wear a sari for the school play. But I wanted an ordinary part in the school play. I did not want to be singled out – like most children, I wanted to be like everyone else; I did not want a culture imposed on me by well-meaning teachers. I did not want to dress up as an Indian doll for the school play, but nobody listened to my pleas so I stood motionless at the front of the stage, tears rolling down my face while bemused teachers watched with no understanding. The tears were my only form of defence – if I was going to be forced into this, I was going to ruin their play and make everyone feel as awkward and unpleasant as I did. It was as if an image existed outside myself that did not belong to me but was judged to be acceptable, a mask and a role, a social norm that had no bearing on who I imagined myself to be. I would like to add that when my adoptive mother died, I wore a sari with enormous pride in memory of her passion and love for India and in memory of my Indian birth mother and father, who I will most probably never be able to meet but to whom I owe my life and of whom I am so very proud.

A while later I was forced to dress up (for a school play) as Girl Friday in a grass skirt and carry a spear. For this humiliation, I won a brush and mirror set that was useless as it was impractical in terms of my thick black hair – the thin blond bristles merely brushed the surface and highlighted my difference even more. I was beyond furious. When I look back on these events it makes me laugh, but as a child I felt deep shame, embarrassment and exclusion. I became withdrawn and hurt, not only because of these experiences but because of the everyday abuses both verbal and physical that I had to endure every time I was in a public space, be that at school or walking to school, visiting friends or walking through the town. I learned at a very young age that the world I lived in was simply not safe, not safe at all.

This book is born out of the lived experience of being BAME in a majority white society and culture. My aim is to create a space for exploration and discovery so that your sense of wellbeing does not hang on other people's expectations, norms, values and behaviours. Inclusion is measured by how you feel, how you are valued, respected recognised and trusted within your environments.

Since the Brexit referendum in 2016, reports of race hate crimes have risen dramatically. There is an increase in the number of racially or religiously aggravated crimes recorded by police in

England and Wales following the referendum. There were 80,393 offences in 2016–17, compared with 62,518 in 2015–16 – the largest increase since the Home Office began recording figures in 2011–12 (Kelly 2007). The recent Race Disparity Audit (Cabinet Office 2017) reveals the sweeping inequalities manifesting themselves throughout the fabric of our society and provides an overall sense of what is going on within our communities.

The discourse has suddenly moved from a vague sense that racism is no longer explicit within our culture (this has not been my own personal experience) to an acknowledgement that it is now implicit; that is, gone underground and not likely to appear as verbal and physical abuse and not so openly pugnacious. Contemporary society as reflected by the media has appeared yet again to shift in relation to race to admit that racism still exists, which of course is something that most BAME people are very much aware of.

'Nobody in this country should have to live their lives enduring fear, intimidation or – in a third of cases – violence because of who they are,' said Mark Hamilton, the National Police Chiefs Council lead on hate crime.[1]

BAME people are still vulnerable to prejudiced attitudes, discriminatory behaviours and levels of exclusion within all elements of society such as the legislative framework in the UK seeks to address. However, as Binna Kandola (2009) observes, although basic principles of anti-discrimination are enshrined in our laws, they are defensive rather than progressive, they do not necessarily guarantee changes in the fabric of our society.

It's fundamental that I address the issue of the language used throughout this book. Language can age at speed, and meanings of words may swing from having a positive to a negative effect. Like many people who are not white, I have struggled with definitions such as Black, Asian and Minority Ethnic and I feel the urge to use the term 'people of colour' (POC) currently being proposed simply because it seems to have crept its way into the language. But my

---

1   www.independent.co.uk/news/uk/crime/brexit-hate-crimes-racism-eu-referendum-vote-attacks-increase-police-figures-official-a7358866.html

understanding is the categorisation POC is limited and open to excluding people such as travellers or migrants from all over the world who have come here and may experience discrimination on the grounds of race, even though they are not visibly different in skin colour. Some commentators would say that the term 'people of colour' erases huge cultural differences and manufactures an alleged sense of solidarity. I tend to agree and feel that this would exclude people who are not visibly of colour but who are of colour since they have mixed heritage, dual heritage or multiple heritage – people whose categorisations seem to be constantly shifting and changing, thus demonstrating how complex and difficult this has become. So, for the purposes of this book and even though it remains unsatisfactory, I will be using the term BAME.

This book is for anyone who is interested in the subject of BAME wellbeing, but predominantly it is written for the hearts and minds of BAME people who may want the opportunity to explore parts of themselves and consider their own realities, their own inner experiences and their own wellbeing. I am making no grand theoretical claims but I am interested in looking at the impact of race and racism on wellbeing. This is not to be problem focused but to explore and be creative in the hope that we may develop new ways of being and living that are less scripted by the current ideological climate. It's clear to me that the most valuable knowledge comes from listening carefully to our own intuitions; time and again we are told to ignore those senses, those intuitive moments where you just know something is not right, and this is because we know racism is in the room in some form or other, even though others may tell you this is not so and that you are being too sensitive and over-reacting. Through our senses, we pick up valuable information and we need to hear it and learn from what it is trying to tell us. We may not want to express these thoughts and feelings; we may wish to keep our own counsel, especially if the counsel of others becomes an invalidating process.

For instance (and this is an experience I would own), surviving trauma in the form of verbal or physical abuse that arises out of discrimination can lead one to become excessively resilient, and to focus on survival and coping skills. This type of resilience can lead to a narrowed-down approach to life and what it has to offer and a hardening of the edges of our being. And yet, it has its uses – again, it is letting us know we are strong, capable and tough, and these are characteristics I embrace as a positive aspect of myself and something I am proud of. Sure, life has not gone in a straight line for me but for most people in the world, as we are witness to, daily life is not straightforward and is full of uncertainty. At the age of 11 I recall walking back from school and facing comments and all kind of verbal assaults shouted from cars and passers-by, most of them adults. Worst of all was being spat on. Being spat on made me feel less than human and disgusted with myself – I almost had to be so dark, so bad, so horrific to others that they needed to defile me in such a physical way. It felt as if I was given up on, as if I had nothing of value to contribute to the world, and I wanted to disappear because if existence was this tough and this horrid, I wanted to get out in some way.

I learned to live with this pain. I learned to hide it because I did not want to be told to ignore it, to defend myself, to be questioned as to whether it happened or to be told it was all in my mind. Even at that age, I knew that these types of conversations with white people would inevitably strip me of my reality, my life, my story, my history and my hurt. These over- and under-reactions were counterproductive to my essence, to my being. Sometimes I would feel that their anger, their outrage at what had happened to me was more important, more listened to and more socially acceptable than mine and I was damned if I was going to share it.

To remain true to myself I kept these everyday abuses to myself so that I could work through them, however inadequately, however maladaptively. I wanted to come out of my life's experience whole and intact and I cannot deny the development of an overly resilient personality. I did not want my energy taken up in moving in to their worlds, trying to make mine a safer place. I wanted to develop a real inner self. I quickly learned that adults did not have all the answers and often made situations worse. I feel as if the only way this book could have been written is because of the resilience I developed, and I receive it with open arms.

I hope this book offers readers new ways of thinking and explaining their unique lives and unique experiences. However much we try to retreat, to deny and disavow, racism still exists in our society and affects individuals in many ways. Unconscious bias is built into the fabric of our society and is not always visible. Conscious bias and explicit bias still exert their hostile influences and are still very visible. Religious hate crime, particularly that of Islamophobia and anti-Semitism, is on the rise in this new, confused and uncertain world that we now inhabit.

I would like to add that I am not somehow miraculously free from prejudice and unexamined thinking but I do feel I have a personal responsibility to keep these things in check, to question my thoughts and challenge myself as much as I am able. There is no single right way, but there is your way.

How a BAME person positions themselves in relation to wellbeing is almost bound to be different from a white person. Issues of 'self-acceptance' for example, are likely to have a focus on colour and identity if you are brought up in a majority white culture. Some BAME people feel unable to fully express psychological distress caused by issues arising from racism because there are few safe spaces to express and explore these areas and few people who are experienced enough to have lived a life that enables them to listen and to hear.

In this book, I would like to invite you to consider the six elements of wellbeing so that BAME people have access to a thinking that places wellbeing high on their own agenda. Drawing on Carol Ryff's (1989) Six-Factor Model of Psychological Wellbeing will offer you a structure and a road map on which to begin the journey. These six factors form the basis for the chapters in this book:

- Self-acceptance and identity

- Environmental mastery

- Positive relations with others

- Autonomy

- Personal growth

- Purpose in life.

Each chapter will offer a reflective space, exercises, observations and sometimes challenges to help you open up a conversation with yourself about what wellbeing means for you and how to build into your life the ways and means of supporting yourself to thrive both emotionally and physically as a BAME person.

While this book will focus on 'race', I fully accept that all our identities overlap and interrelate. How people develop and experience their racial identity is interconnected with other aspects of their identity. It has become increasingly clear that racial identity cannot be understood as separate from other identities and that these are complex and interrelate. Intersectional theory maintains that we have many social identities which simultaneously interact and affect our experiences and it is these combinations that mutually shape each other. While some identities may be more prominent at different times, all of them are part of who we are and how we experience and make sense of the world.

How might it feel if you were a gay black man in your 60s who had not 'come out' in 2017? What is life like as a BAME man with a disability or a BAME woman in a senior role within an organisation coming from a high socio-economic background? People will experience levels of power and powerlessness depending on the context and their intersectionality. Race can come to the fore in any context. This book is written from a race-centred, single identity focus (Wijeyessinghe and Jackson, 2001, p.219). But it is well worth considering your identity among numerous other social categories (such as race, ethnicity, sex, gender, class, age, religion). Which groups do you consider most central to who you are and how do these identities affect your experiences, opportunities, sense of self and world view?

The importance of these identities varies in the way in which they interact among individuals. A single identity approach asks the question: What does it mean to be a member of a racial group? – but not what does it mean to be a member of a racial group and to be 80 instead of 12. Or to be non- religious or to be a Muslim.

It may be that your race and class are more important concerns for you to work through, or it may be that your religion and cultural issues have more significance in your current life circumstances.

Clearly, the issue of intersectionality in respect of the above is extremely significant and not to be ignored, but for the purposes of this book we will remain within a single identity approach as a starting point.

I have made the decision to use the category BAME (Black, Asian and Minority Ethnic) mainly because I find some of the other terminology problematic but I also accept that the term BAME separates and leaves us questioning and confused about who/what is an ethnic minority. This marking out is the cause of much confusion both to me and, I imagine, to you, the reader. I'm left with the use of the term simply because it the one I hear most commonly used by other BAME people.

Over the past 20 years, in both professional and volunteering roles, I have had the experience of working with a diverse population in many different settings. I have encountered noticeable themes and patterns, and to reflect these themes I have blended material from many sources and presented them as a single case. Protecting client confidentiality is the cornerstone of any counselling work, so details have been drawn from multiple cases and merged into one, and as such are non-identifiable.

Within the chapters of the book I have added 'pause buttons'. These are spaces for reflective thinking and understanding. To guide you on your journey, I have included some exercises at the end of each chapter. These spaces and exercises are aimed at increasing your choices and options (instead of perhaps narrowing your view of the 'self') and exploring new ways of thinking and feeling.

Talking about race is a demanding and challenging conversation to have with others and with oneself. It can be filled with intense and powerful emotions that may feel threatening and uncomfortable. The aim of this book is to enable you to get closer to the subject and have the conversation with yourself and with others that makes a difference to your wellbeing, and to rediscover or shine a light on a new perspective that allows for growth, self-acceptance and change.

I hope this will also provide you with some guidance and a means of managing difficult incidents, microaggressions and micro-inequalities that can be expressions of discrimination and prejudice and go to make up some of today's 'modern racism'.

Diversification and inclusivity are merely words holding little meaning unless we understand that we need to move towards social justice together so that lived equality can appear on all our horizons. We are all in need of profound change.

Chapter **1**

SELF-ACCEPTANCE AND IDENTITY

◐ *Identity and self-acceptance:* These come about when you possess a positive attitude towards yourself, acknowledge and accept multiple aspects of yourself, including both good and bad qualities, and feel positive about your earlier life. Your identity will most likely be formed because of various personal experiences you have had from family, peers, significant others, your environment, work, school, life and culture.

◐ *Low self-acceptance:* This means that you feel dissatisfied with yourself, are disappointed with what has occurred in your earlier life, are troubled about certain personal qualities and wish to be different from what and who you are.

This chapter attempts to explore 'race' and 'racial identity', enabling you to discover how your identity is accomplished in everyday interactions. Becoming more conscious of your identity will support your wellbeing and your resilience. Identity can act as a protective shield, triggering a sense of belonging to a community, or building an internal sense of pride. Identity is accomplished in everyday interactions and is therefore constantly in the making.

What wellbeing is and is not

The concept of wellbeing is on the one hand tangible, in that there are practical and objective steps you can take to take care of yourself and enhance your general health, and on the other hand also difficult to pin down in some sense because it is highly subjective and personal. What might be important for one person may not be for another. What might be important in one culture may not be in another.

Carol Ryff's (1989) Model of Psychological Wellbeing is multi-dimensional. It is not merely about happiness or positive emotions, but about building a 'good life' that is balanced, whole and engaging instead of being narrowly focused on attaining the feel-good factor.

Martin Seligman (2011), in his book *Flourish,* describes wellbeing as being like the weather – there are facets to it that cannot be defined by one thing. The weather is not rain or sunshine, it is a combination of different elements and interactions between them, it is not fixed. Similarly, when getting to grips with our wellbeing, it is helpful to take our emotional temperature, to check in with ourselves, to notice what is happening for us both internally and externally, make meaningful choices, and take conscious action where we can.

The way in which you view yourself and how you hold conversations with yourself can both increase and decrease your sense of wellbeing. So it follows that building a strong sense of identity will increase your strength and resilience and help you to stay on track in the face of adversities (Gibbs 1988; Neff and Germer 2018; Seligman 2011).

The meaning of identity
Exploring a BAME identity

Identity might be thought of as a part of us that is constantly in the making – by this I mean, it is not static, it changes from moment to moment and alongside your personal experiences and your social context. Your identity includes your distinguishing characteristics, personality and individuality, as well as what separates and connects you in your social contexts. At certain times, we choose our identity, and at other times it might feel as if our identity chooses us. For example, as a child you may have gone to school in a multicultural community where you felt at ease with your identity. On visiting a less diverse community you may feel your identity is now thrown against a different background (Rankine 2014). In a new setting, you may be perceived as strange and alien and this may be pointed out to you in the form of staring, curiosity, touching and intrusive curiosity.

We adapt the way we see ourselves depending on our circumstances: where we are, who we are with and what we are trying to achieve.

Identity is used to describe the way you define yourself on a personal level and the way in which you are defined by society at large. Who you are, the way you think about yourself and the way you are viewed by other people has a strong impact on self-acceptance. As such, your identity is based on a range of factors:

- Culture

- Family background

- Community

- Education

- Language

- Social activities

- Economic ability

- Skin colour

- Hair.

How you define yourself and what gives your life meaning is hugely important in relation to the factors listed above. Allowing yourself to be positive about your identity is crucial to holding on to a positive sense of wellbeing and to developing resilience. In a post-Brexit society, how BAME individuals enact their identity dominates the social and political landscape. For example, Wijeyesinghe and Jackson (2001) introduce the concept that in order to fulfil critical needs, wants and desires such as employment, education, banking, shopping and accessing medical care, BAME individuals must enter, and perform confidently within, mainstream institutions that make up the dominant culture. They go on to suggest that the rules and conventions for how to enter, act, dress, speak and perform within this culture are generally influenced by mainstream norms. BAME identity, therefore, must include the capacity to 'code switch' – a form of identity switching, perspective taking, and multi-cultural competence. Examples of code switching might be: toning down an accent; using different cultural references, such as music and literature; wearing hair and clothes differently with the overall aim of fitting in creatively and responsively while adapting to different environments. This means developing a great deal of flexible emotional resilience that goes mostly unrecognised as being adaptable and open to modifying and adjusting one's behaviour in various settings and against various cultural backdrops.

In positive psychology, self-esteem has long been considered an element of psychological good health. Self-esteem can be defined as how we feel about ourselves and who we are in the world, often in comparison to others. We are frequently given advice in the media and self-help books on how to raise our self-esteem and conquer low self-esteem, often in ways to feel better fast with cheerful 'post-it note' optimism.

There is nothing inherently 'wrong' with this; however, in an age of digital dominance and access to the curated inner lives and musings of what feels like the world's population – 24 hours a day – deciphering the many overt and covert messages about how we should function as a human being can leave us in a state of compare and despair. Often these messages are carriers of the norms and values of the dominant culture, which may not resonate with you.

We are challenged to define ourselves in daily conversations that are now well documented as forms of 'microaggressions' and of 'othering':

- Who are you?

- Where are you from?

- Why are you here?

The motivation and underlying reasons for asking these questions are varied and might result as a consequence of: naive curiosity, feelings of being under threat from something that is different, a clumsy form of reaching out to make a connection, an unconscious bias that insists on pocketing this knowledge to shore up stereotypes, and so on. It's interesting to note the same knowledge is rarely sought from white people with such intense determination.

Building a strong sense of identity will increase your competence when managing covert or overt forms of race-based discrimination.

Definitions will be imposed on us if we don't know the answers to the questions presented above. Afua Hirsch, in her fantastically powerful book *Brit(ish)*, reflects on this:

> Belonging is a foundational human need. For most people, throughout most of history, it was inherited from family, shaped by society, and contained within language, customs, religion, and nationhood, in an unconscious process of social conditioning. That's not to say that these identities aren't frequently disrupted, dispersed, updated – that's as much a part of the human condition as the need to belong. (2018, p.22)

Without clear and consciously formed answers we will be left vulnerable to subtle forms of discrimination and othering. And your feelings of wellbeing will fluctuate, emotions will vary, because your thoughts and responses and those of others will influence your mood. This is normal; it does not mean the foundation of your wellbeing and identity cannot be solid and hold you securely when you feel vulnerable or directionless or when you face ignorance, bias and oppression.

Developing and constructing a comfortable identity and one that fits your unique lived experience is an important and ongoing process. Being able to voice that identity and stand by that identity in the face of race-based experiences is an essential survival skill.

A personal perspective

I will always be me. I feel like me, I am me, but my racial identity has shifted and changed over time and I feel that I have become more flexible in my personal approach to identity. I have become more accepting of others and of myself and am less caught up in internal struggles. It is as if I have formed and shaped my identity over many years and alongside this I have been slowly reclaiming my individual power.

Immersing myself in the struggle for social justice left little time for developing other opportunities and the space to explore other aspects of my identity. I became lost in a collective anger that was justifiably played out in the political activism of the time. As a consequence, I neglected other important areas of my life, particularly my health and wellbeing. Now, and with hindsight, I have made the decision to step back from political movements because sometimes it's just plain exhausting. To be overwhelmed and immersed in continuous activism and struggle is simply not a big enough life for me at this moment in time.

The decisions I am making are complex and ongoing. Nowadays I consciously make choices; I haven't let things happen to me or be 'done' to me because of the colour of my skin. Where possible, I try to step back and give myself time to make autonomous choices, allowing spaces for previously neglected aspects of myself to flourish.

Nevertheless, the act of striving for race equality and for social justice has been a huge part of my life. I have chosen to throw my energy into writing this book in the hope that it will offer new ways of processing and thinking about race and its links to identity, to wellbeing and the journey towards building resilience.

Navigating different identities is complex and challenging. We exist in spaces where 'bad things' happen, and these factors are often out of our control. Looking after ourselves in every aspect of life and in all areas where we can exert some influence, even in the smallest of ways, will improve our wellbeing and resilience.

Language: new and emerging identities

Reni Eddo-Lodge (2017), in the preface to *Why I'm No Longer Talking to White People About Race*, has a word to say about the use of definitions. She decided to use three terms throughout her book. First, 'people of colour' (POC) to define anyone of any race who is not white; second, 'black' to describe people of African Caribbean heritage, including mixed race people; and finally, a reluctant use of the term Black and Minority Ethnic as a necessity due to its reliance within methods of research. In her marvellously uncompromising piece of work, Eddo-Lodge inevitably grapples with the use of categorisations as we move into a far more complex social set of circumstances.

Rajdeep Sandhu's headline (May 2018) also speaks of this complexity: 'Should BAME be ditched as a term for black, Asian and minority ethnic people?' The conversation centres round the problems with labelling different people under one category and giving undue prominence to one single categorisation. In the same article David Lammy, MP, writes that the term BAME is 'lazy and a piece of jargon', going on to argue for a more American style approach that draws on a person's heritage, for example, African American, Italian American or Asian American.

The article concludes by asking if young people identify with these types of categorisations. Several people were interviewed holding contrasting views. Some suggested that these kinds of terms under-represent or misrepresent because they group people altogether with no differentiation, but this begs the question, what could we replace it with? Others expressed an acceptance that BAME is a good umbrella term for people who are not BAME but not for people who are! And finally, there was a suggestion that an overarching term like this promotes solidarity.

Reducing unique experiences under a 'one size fits all' category undoubtedly constrains BAME identity. In my view, the term BAME is merely functional and useful in relation to the collection of data (ethnic monitoring forms) rather than in providing real connections to any personal thoughts and feelings about identity. We are still in a position where we need to be able to collect data regarding disparities within all areas of life in the UK. We would do ourselves an injustice to let go of the protection that race equalities legislation has brought us over the last 50 years and the data it has provided. So, from my point of view, I feel stuck with the term BAME.

I agree with Colin Lago that categorisation of different groups in society is a problematic process and 'in terms of both culture and race, contemporary Britain serves to reveal a population that has a myriad of origins and a huge range of subcultures' (1996, p.1). As a consequence, we are left struggling with how to categorise new and emerging identities and I have the same lack of ease with the terminology BAME, but despite this I am using it for the purposes of this book.

Learning how to build a positive sense of race and identity

Recent theories in sociology see identity as fluid, linked to the way in which people connect and relate to place, as with the example of Eshe.

CASE STUDY

Eshe is a 16-year-old woman who feels she cannot relate to categorisations such as BAME, African Caribbean or people of colour and refers to herself as 'Urban' which relates to her city life (place), the diverse people she mixes with (connectedness), her generation (fluidity) and her peer group. Eshe and her friends are responding to the ongoing problems with the application of categorisations. Their approach has shelved what is perceived as outdated terminology for a new urban generation that is seeking out new definitions of identity.

Passively accepting hand-me-down roles and outdated identities, because that it what the generations have done before, will inevitably diminish a sense of wellbeing because we won't have an owned sense of identity and will remain lost in the shadows of what has gone before.

Identities have been fought for and history has seen off words like 'coloured' – offensive terminology associated with the era of segregationist politics of the United States. This appeared as both acceptable in the UK in the 1960s and 70s as a category, and unacceptable and heavily used as a term of abuse.

Pressure from family, peer group, work and school may prevent us from making choices about how we define ourselves, but it is nevertheless worthwhile making conscious choices that can be saved for a later date or when you are in circumstances where the pressures are non-existent.

Facing the challenges of race-related incidents and their impact on our everyday lives is psychologically demanding and may lead us to holding on to safer identities. This chapter is not about judging anyone's decision making but it is about opening up new conversations and examining new possibilities.

Each of us has our own lived experience of race and racism, and how this impacts on our everyday lives is a unique and individual journey. Nonetheless, living in a majority white culture will almost certainly affect aspects of your identity. How you experience your race and how you experience racism will also affect your sense of wellbeing.

Race and identity

Race and racism is a major factor/aspect that affects identity, particularly if your environment is made up of a majority that is white.

The need for identification and a sense of belonging is an important emotional issue for everyone. Racism is based on an ideology which assumes the superiority and inferiority of people according to race, and it is proving very resistant to change. We belong to a group that is socially stigmatised and the object of discrimination. Learning to come to terms with the significance of race and racism is a lifelong journey. Managing your wellbeing in the face of discrimination also takes a lifetime and there are no easy fixes.

Exploring your identity offers a chance to gain insight in understanding your connection with your experience of race and race-related incidents. It might also act as a guide and a reference point, enabling you to link your individual experience to other BAME experiences.

So, for example, perhaps a healthy BAME identity would accept, understand and acknowledge experiences related to race, processing these rather than ignoring or denying their existence.

We are often presented with difficult and complex choices; if you were brought up in a family where religious beliefs were central, you may decide to retain and celebrate certain values and beliefs belonging to that religion. Or perhaps you may decide to break from your family traditions completely, with an understanding that it is 'not your way'.

Denying race-based experiences is a means of survival and perfectly normal in certain contexts, but as you go through life you may find this approach becomes redundant – because race does matter and the issues it raises will not go away.

In developing new confidence, you may learn to accept aspects of yourself you have previously cast aside. The case study below illustrates the complexity of this journey for some young people.

CASE STUDY

Adam is a 12-year-old boy whose parents are Malaysian. Adam is being brought up within a Buddhist background. At school, he never speaks about his parents' beliefs or his ethnicity. To get by with his peers he jokes about people who come from his background and does not use his Malaysian name. He switches identities between his home life and family culture, his school mates who are all white, and his British Malaysian friends. He has become an expert in switching his cultural identity on a daily basis.

Adam appears to be uncomfortable expressing aspects of his ethnic identity or culture outside his home. He also seems to reject aspects of himself and adhere at least publicly to negative stereotypes surrounding his identity. The most likely effect of this behaviour will be that it will undermine his sense of wellbeing when he falls in with jokes about his race. This is essentially detrimental to how he views himself, and the resulting costs may be shame and guilt. However, he is also undeniably flexible and resilient in his ability to maintain inclusion on both sides of this divide. He is able to speak in two voices and access two identities at the same time.

Similarly, you may also have encountered situations where you choose aspects of different cultural identities. For example, you may have been raised in a family where modern arranged marriages (not the same as a forced marriage) are expected; where the prospective bride or groom has a lot more say over who they will eventually marry. Even this may personally represent a lack of autonomy and you may want to opt out of this tradition and choose your own partner.

Separating yourself from your parents' values and beliefs is a process I would not underestimate within any culture. These are age-old and emotionally challenging struggles for independence that can be very painful and sometimes impossible to enact, and they happen within all cultures.

Awareness of your own values and beliefs is a necessary starting point because it enables you to become clearer about your own world view, which your parents may not share. It is also a means of taking more responsibility for your life, having control, building resilience and becoming self-aware, all of which contribute towards health and wellbeing.

As Georgina Lawton (2017) sums up in her article, 'Living on the borderline: how I embraced my mixed-race status after years of denial':

> For me, having something of a complex identity as a mixed-race woman leaves me with so much room to choose what to embrace and what to reject. There's a certain freedom in not quite belonging to English or Irish, white or black, and picking little pieces from each.

Navigating a mixed-race identity can prove difficult and emotionally complicated; it would be reasonable to identify as much with a white heritage as that of a black one. Making the decision to lean towards one or the other or of finding a place somewhere in between can take its toll and make its demands. Integration is a process that involves combining one thing with another to form a whole. Therefore, accepting multiple aspects of ourselves is a process of integration that enables us to become stronger and more confident in controlling our lives and building resilience. In the case study below, Aisha's personal journey through integration is in contrast to that of her sister's.

CASE STUDY

Aisha comes from a mixed-race family. She likes to describe herself as mixed heritage and feels proud of her identity, although her sister, who is lighter in skin colour than she is, has never mentioned the issue of race and they have never spoken about it. In some ways, Aisha feels hurt by her approach and feels as if her sister is rejecting not only a part of herself but a part of her. Their parents avoid talking about it and it is never brought up in conversations.

Inclusive identities

How you identify must be your choice, but even so, the impact of that choice may be difficult for you on many levels. The example of Aisha and her sister highlights the complexities people face. Aisha's sister, being lighter in skin colour, might never have to face discrimination because she is not seen as visibly BAME. However, she has a different set of problems to contend with: first, she may feel some sense of guilt and shame that her sister has encountered racism, and second, she might fear being targeted herself. The two approaches given here are one-dimensional but nevertheless demonstrate some of the complexity surrounding integration.[1]

Complications may also arise in connecting with your identity if you are mixed race and are raised by a white parent and a BAME parent. For example, it may perhaps reinforce a sense of confusion, lead to feeling misunderstood or to feeling a general lack of a sense of belonging. Most children will inevitably take into considerations their parents' thoughts and feelings about how they might identify, and this consideration might create tensions between family members who feel strongly as to how they identify. The choices we make occur in a context of family, community, social and work environments and within society.

Some studies support the opinion of mixed race people as troubled and confused with their identity and yet other studies reinforce that there are no psychological differences compared to mono-racial peers, contesting the myth that mixed race individuals are confused and disturbed (Wijeyesinghe and Jackson 2001). More research is needed, and my own experience of working with mixed race clients has continuously thrown up themes around managing the complex nature of such identities.

In her article, Georgina Lawton (2017) states:

We're asked to split ourselves in two, to align ourselves with one side more than the other. If we don't, we are accused of

---

1   I use the term 'mixed race', but individuals identify themselves as bi-racial, dual heritage, mixed parentage, and so on.

deliberately trying to obscure a part of ourselves, when really we are still just trying to work out how to embrace it all.

However, research has identified experiences that are unique to being 'mixed race', such as having one's racial identity become a source of controversy. Having one's identity regularly questioned is another example of the way in which microaggressions are apportioned to BAME individuals who are consigned to spending time and energy facing these kinds of everyday encounters.

In order to survive life's circumstances, sometimes people may minimise aspects of their identity, downplaying it in order to navigate their environments. Psychological protection against the effects of race-based discrimination may be achieved through various means, such as confrontation, challenge, avoidance, passivity or passive aggressive behaviour. The recipient of discrimination is left with few options other than to find ways of managing complex and problematic responses that diminish their sense of ease within their lived experiences.

Learning to accept different identities

Disowning race-related experiences, avoiding any membership or identity alliance to BAME groups or denying the existence of racism within the current British context may well place you at risk. Wishing to avoid the issue of race-related experiences is understandable and may arise out of feelings of powerlessness, confusion, lack of awareness, fear, shame and, most powerfully, not having the tools to defend yourself and hence internalising your experiences.

By way of illustration, Alleyne (2004) speaks of the internal oppressor:

> which is the process of absorbing consciously or unconsciously the values and beliefs of the oppressor and subscribing to the stereotypes and misinformation about one's group, at least in part. Such a process leads to low self-esteem, self-hate, the disowning of one's own group, and other complex defensive interpersonal behaviours that influence and impair quality of life.

Being prepared, rehearsed and making plans in a practical and psychological sense for the experience of racism is healthy and beneficial. Difficult feelings, thoughts and emotions are likely to arise out of an experience of racism, so knowing where to access the most appropriate support is fundamental.

By contrast, there will be some BAME people who might have escaped any form of race-based discrimination. You are not wrong for not having experienced racism. As a consequence, your experience will be different because you have experienced your world as a safe environment. At the same time, it remains useful to develop the ability to manage and cope with race-based experiences and encounters – a naive optimism will not support you in any event – and preparation for negative experiences within the dominant culture is well worth exploring. Increasing awareness and an understanding of how others experience race-based discrimination is valuable to us all.

In March 2018, the Mayor of London, Sadiq Khan, publicly revealed a string of social media messages from people who were intent on defining him as less than human. The dehumanisation of BAME people is a deeply rooted instrument of oppression. But the fact that we have a Mayor of London brave enough to speak out constitutes a new dialogue around race-based hate crime in the UK. Such hate crimes can have the effect of discouraging young people from having anything to do with public life and being wary of a public platform. Sadiq Khan has made a strong commitment to encourage and empower people to have a voice, even though he must realise as soon as he posted the video that the threats would increase. We cannot all be as brave as this and nor should we feel pressured into doing so, but it represents a multi-cultural Britain that we can be proud of.

Sadiq Khan's experience illustrates that revealing race-based crime carries risk to personal safety. BAME people learn from a very young age that it's not always safe to stand up for yourself when you fear being labelled a troublemaker or being too sensitive. And, as adults understand from their lived experience, this type of labelling is predictable and accepted as part of their everyday lives. There are clearly hidden pitfalls in raising your head above the parapet, but in spite of this, being able to predict and prepare for difficulties is one way of coping and managing race-based discrimination.

That being the case, often the outward expression and vulnerability of BAME people can be problematic and may possibly lead to a rigid controlling of emotions or, worse, a feeling that you have no right to those emotions. The feelings generated are frequently denied in a white majority context, and blame is transferred to the victim with the familiar cry that it is they who have the chip on their shoulders.

The experience of standing up for yourself

'I think I said too much', 'I was too aggressive', 'I spoke too strongly', 'I'm worried about my job and I am worried how I will be perceived.' These are phrases all too often heard when BAME people are defending a position or defending their human rights and asking for the dignity and respect they deserve. Championing a position by speaking out may well produce a negative response. This may cause people to adapt, become passive, silencing the self and becoming bystanders to their own abuse. Watching without involvement because it makes for a so-called easier life is adapting your identity to fit into uncomfortable and invalidating spaces.

Accordingly, standing up for yourself is likely to get you labelled as a troublemaker, a radical, a complainer, an activist, quirky, a dramatist and a rebel. It is often a lifelong learning process to overcome other people's labels, but it is one worth pursuing rather than turning the labelling and stereotyping against yourself.

The difficulty is that both adaptions – over-expressing and supressing – arise out of an external pressure of something beyond our control.

Identity and physical appearance

Much has been written about the impact of skin colour and hair on the lives of BAME people. Constant comments about hair and skin colour invade personal space and breach the boundaries afforded to others, making up another form of microaggression.

I don't think I could write about racism without mentioning the impact that hair has on the lives of BAME people. Hair is one of the most obviously visible differences and one can be identified as BAME from the texture and colour of one's hair, so in this sense it is a marker of difference and therefore oppression. BAME men and women are instantly called out as different because of their hair.

Natural hairstyles are under attack, particularly in terms of the use of hair dye which seems to have become endemic in society. Hair that is non-western is often perceived as strange, too 'ethnic', unprofessional or an outright challenge to the norms and values of British society. Hair can even be a signifier of militancy and anger.

We remain in a culture where women and men are continually made to feel that they are only attractive if they match up to beauty standards that are paraded before us, and we are held ransom to the consumer culture that is the god of our time; it demands much of us, especially when the standard is pale skin and straight hair. This is poignantly summed up in one sentence: 'My hair grows out rather than down' (Shukla 2016).

The reality is that most of the world's populations have very different types of hair that involve the use and abuse of very different products. Since ancient times, African men and women have braided, oiled, twisted, decorated and patterned their hair for many different reasons and to signify many different aspects of their lives and traditions. This begs the question, are we emulating white people or fighting for social acceptance and to be viewed equally? Or are we trying to live up to a simply unachievable white standard?

The 1960s gave rise to three words 'black is beautiful'. Hair became a key determinant in visually declaring black pride. Hairstyle became indicative of one's politics and straightening hair perceived as almost blasphemous. In both the UK and the United States, the 1970s gave rise to the use of braids and weaves. Now we need to consider where the hair to make those extensions and weaves originates (Byrd and Tharps 2001). According to Khaleeli (2012), 'Much of the hair on sale comes from small agents who tour villages in India, China, and Eastern Europe, offering poverty-stricken women small payments to part with their hair.'

We are still living in the grip of slavery, the giant precursor of post-industrialisation, with mass consumerism its legacy. We still inhabit the post-colonial world and until power dramatically shifts from 'west is better than the rest', we are going to continue to be left living up to unattainable standards. Because if we don't fit in, if we don't at least try to look like a white person, then our lives are full of threats and obstacles nigh impossible to overcome on our own.

If you are discriminated against because of your visible difference from the majority population you will be constantly reminded by words and deeds, from microaggressions and unconscious behaviours that you are from the 'outgroup'. Oughts and shoulds imposed from the outside (particularly the media) serve to decrease and diminish a strong sense of one's own identity: 'For not only must the black man be black; he must be black in relation to the white man' (Fanon 1961, p.219).

In other words, we are not in a position of being a human being, we cannot speak for the commonality of humanity. We can speak for our race and we do speak of our race, even when we do not wish to do so.

Below is a reflection allowing you to explore your own identity. Accurate feedback is crucial to self-learning, and providing yourself with accurate feedback is a skill that can be developed. Reflective writing and reflective self-talk help to minimise negative automatic thinking and help you see what other factors may have played a part in a situation. Calm reflection helps to bring in a wider perspective and combats over-personalisation, where you may feel compelled to take responsibility for something that is not directly within your control or you have been handed this responsibility whether it is yours or not to accept.

REFLECTION POINTS

Exploring your own identity:

○ How would you describe your identity?

○ How would you describe yourself as a BAME person?

○ Do you have other aspects you wish to add?

○ Who influenced your identity?

○ How do you feel about being BAME?

Imagine waking up one morning and walking down the road as a white person:

○ What would you have lost?

○ What would have changed, if anything?

○ How do you imagine it might feel?

Aisha Dupont-Joshua, a therapist who has written extensively on working inter-culturally in counselling settings, poses the question: What would it feel like being one of the majority, being historically dominant, having access to privilege, being part of what is considered aesthetically attractive and being in control (Palmer 2002).

The key to wellbeing is to understand yourself and to take notice of your identity, as it has an enormous influence on your experiences. There are real differences between groups of people and we are entitled to explore these. The habit of checking in with yourself is a powerful vehicle for self-care and self-nurturing when society offers everyday complex challenges. As with any habit, it takes practice, perseverance and patience to embed newly discovered awareness and follow this through into our daily life; however, if you can begin to create opportunities for positive identity you will be making an investment in your wellbeing and life satisfaction that is immeasurable.

In his book *Learning by Doing*, Professor Graham Gibbs (1988) developed the Reflective Cycle, which helps you to look at a situation objectively and take into account your thoughts, feelings and actions for the future. Using this model of reflection can help you to process an experience and take something tangible from it. BAME people are often challenged to define themselves and this is now well documented as the 'where do you come from conversations'. These are considered to be a form of microaggression. Working through such incidents using the Reflective Cycle will help you to balance yourself, heal from the confrontation and bounce back.

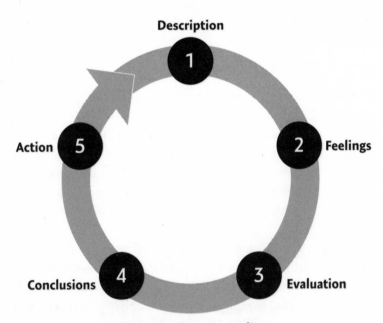

Figure 1.1: Your surroundings

Asking questions related to each area and exploring how you feel and think about a difficult situation from a bit of a distance can help to achieve closure on a relationship, for example, or to consider how you would approach a potential confrontation in the future.

Questions you could pose include:

- *Description* – What happened? Who was there? What was said?

- *Feelings* – How did I feel in the situation? How did I respond to how I felt? Was I responding to anyone else's expectations of me?

- *Evaluation* – What did I decide to do or say in the moment? Would I do anything differently next time?

- *Conclusion* – How do I feel now? What was within my control and what wasn't?

- *Action* – What do I want to do now? What do I want to do in the future? What might I change, if anything?

Once you have written up or internally reflected on these questions, revisit them sometime later and evaluate anew how you feel about the situation now. This helps to mirror back to you what remains important and what is no longer relevant, or that you no longer need invest that level of emotion in it. This practice can help you to balance out and heal from events that, left unprocessed, may remain with you in a confusing and painful way, impacting on your wellbeing and resilience.

Racial and cultural identity development model

Feeling good about who we are enables us to respect and value others; for this reason, achieving a healthy sense of racial identity is important to our sense of wellbeing. Respecting and valuing others begins with respecting and valuing yourself.

A range of models of identity development have been established in the United States. In brief, these models seek to illustrate the process human beings may move through in their search for identity. These models provide a framework from which to explore identity. They can, of course, be criticised for generalising and simplifying the complexity surrounding the issue of identity and its possible lack of reference to a British context. Despite these reservations, they do at least provide a useful set of ideas that generate 'meaning making' and new ways of thinking as well as offering a different perspective on facing the challenges arising out of the BAME experience.

It could be said that rather than stages with distinct boundaries, we could think of identity development as woven into the fabric of our relationships, our sense of self and the places in which we exist.

As an example of a framework for exploring identity, I have adapted and combined these stages taken from Wijeyesinghe and Jackson (2001).

Stage 1 – Fitting in (naivity)

- Identifying with dominant cultural values and absorbing the idea that whiteness equals superiority, normality, beauty and status.

- Lack of awareness of your own identity.

- Negativity towards self and others and only a vague awareness of individual and institutional racism.

- Acceptance and belief in dominant group stereotypes, such as thinking that you don't belong to a racial group.

- Personal dislike (for example, negative feelings about your BAME identity).

Stage 2 – Confusion/uncomfortable feelings (acceptance)

- Confusion and conflict about previously held values. You are unable to express your unique identity. You still feel a sense that you need to gain approval and self-worth by living your life in keeping with the status quo but feeling uncomfortable when doing so. You are left juggling the expectations of the dominant culture. You learn to view yourself through the prism of whiteness, accepting white culture boundaries and values as if they were your own.

- Increased awareness of racism, sexism and oppression. You may have previously shrugged off media messages about racism, viewing these as isolated incidents that don't affect you personally. In the light of new information, or new connections, or even because you have witnessed a friend dealing with racism that has profoundly affected you, you begin to come to terms with the view that racism is interwoven into the fabric of our society and at this point you have shifted your perspective.

- Anger and loss in search of your own role models.

Stage 3 – Opposing (resistance)

- Active reflection and distrust of dominant culture. You begin to be far more aware of the impact of racism. Normal feelings such as hurt, pain and anger are felt to be legitimate responses to your experiences past and present.

- Greater identification with your own culture. You embrace aspects of BAME culture simply because it is not white, and in opposition to whiteness.

- Immersion into your own culture such as your own group history.

- Traditions, food and language.

- Activist/political behaviour such as challenging oppression. You may be entering a phase where you feel overwhelmed with anger and begin to overtly challenge racism.

- Wish to separate from dominant culture. In the past, you may have chosen a path of least resistance but you are realising this is no longer sustainable.

- Strong feelings of hatred and disdain for white people.

Stage 4 – Contemplation (redefinition)

- Self-questioning of rigid rejection of dominant group values while retaining your focus on BAME culture. You are no longer reacting in response to white institutions and culture.

- Conflict and confusion about loyalty to your own cultural group.

- Increasing autonomy of self. What has become important to you is the 'claiming and 'reclaiming' of key elements of BAME culture. The rejection of whiteness is not the focus of self-discovery.

- Struggles with self-awareness and facing uncomfortable feelings.

Stage 5 – Multiculturally inclusive

- As a multi-culturalist you are connected to many groups, such as Asian, white, Chinese, Black, African Caribbean.

- Resolution of personal conflict. You no longer feel the need to explain, defend, or protect your identity in the light of experiences carried forward into this stage.

- Sense of fulfilment with personal and cultural identity. You begin to understand the importance of nurturing a sense of your own uniqueness.

- Appreciation of other cultural groups as well as dominant group values. You begin to be aware of your own intersectional approach – translating into the idea that you become more aware of how being BAME also relates to your being a man or a woman, to your social class, your ableism or disability and your sexual identity.

- Motivation to eliminate all forms of oppression.

- A strong, positive sense of who you are and you understand the prejudices and discrimination that are experienced by other groups of people.

In her book, *Being White in the Helping Professions*, Judy Ryde (2009) has devised a White Identity Model. This cyclical model shows the process which can lead to white people becoming more aware of their white privilege, owning their part in the privilege and leading to acceptance, and, as a consequence of acceptance, going on to naturally act in the world in a way that, as far as possible, does not perpetuate the situation.

REFLECTION POINTS

◑ Do you relate to any of these stages?

◑ Have you encountered thoughts and feelings you recognise from the model?

◑ What else comes into play for you and your own development of self?

For some people, identity development is an intense internal struggle. Aiming for perfection, resolution or a fixed identity ought not to be the destination. Nevertheless, exploring identity supports further understanding of how we experience race-based discrimination and identity-related microaggressions.

Intersectionality and other social identities

Intersectionality represents unchartered territory and implies a readiness to handle complexity: 'It maintains that we have many social identities which simultaneously interact and affect our experiences of power and privilege' (Wijeyesinghe and Jackson 2001, p.216).

It begs the question: What does it mean for a BAME person who is of an ethnic group, has a specific gender expression, is of a particular social class and a particular age, all of which contribute to the term 'intersectionality?'

All of these identities are a part of who we are and are reflected in our lived experiences and everyday lives. Seeing identity through the lens of intersectionality provides us with a challenge and these challenges can be seen, for example, in the recent struggles by BAME lesbian, gay, bisexual and trans (LGBT) movements which have felt excluded, and where other movements have failed to recognise that BAME individuals may primarily feel united by their experience of racial inequality within social movements such as feminism, socialism and liberalism. As Reni Eddo-Lodge (2017, p.27) says: 'Much of the feminist movement's interest in BAME women is not a concern with racism, but a proclaiming of sisterhood with all the women of the world – validating a principle that patriarchy is the fundamental oppression.'

New ways of thinking about racial identity may emerge as generations of young people assert their unique selves in contexts previously unimaginable, for example the campaign 'Walking Black'. 'Walking while black' is an expression referring to the racial profiling of black pedestrians, using a play on words derived from the United States' criminal offence of driving while intoxicated. Variations of the phrase now include 'driving while black', 'learning while black', 'shopping while black' and 'eating while black'.

Understanding your own racial identity promotes self-awareness as well as an appreciation of other people's realities, and there are many factors that contribute to a sense of BAME identity. These arise out of your cultural background and your everyday lived experience.

The decision to give greater attention to race and to put aside the issue of intersectionality arose because our starting point is to grasp the complexity of the experience of race and wellbeing rather than intersectionality and wellbeing. Some of this book will guide you towards a better understanding of intersectionality, while the focus remains on race.

Wijeyesinghe and Jackson (2001, p.219) offer a developmental framework to approaching the intersectional journey from a race-centred single identity focus through to a full intersectional focus.

This describes a journey towards increased awareness of intersectionality, for example a BAME woman experiences an incident of harassment in her workplace and may interpret it as a race-centred single identity focus rather than thinking about her gender in this context. Using the same example, a full intersectional analysis of this incident might include gender, class and specific racial background.

A race-centred, limited intersectional focus provides us with a starting point in an approach to BAME wellbeing. However, we would not want to ignore the distinctiveness and importance of different identities by 'placing race at the heart of the inquiry' (Wijeyesinghe and Jackson 2001, p.221). Even with a race-centred approach, we can still set a context which recognises other social identities and forms of oppression, and the ways in which they interact and intersect. There resides even now an idea of 'colour blindness' which denies the existence of race and racism. A stronger grounding in the BAME experience is a foundation on which to build, even though the relation to other social identities is doubtless inseparable.

Racial identity is shaped by time and context (Wijeyesinghe and Jackson 2001). As individuals, it's worth bearing in mind that we may define our identity but this may differ from the way we are seen by others. Having a lived BAME experience affects one's behaviours, attitudes, values and world view in a myriad of ways.

Racism occurs on different levels:

- Individual

- Institutional

- Societal

- Cultural.

The BAME experience affects one's opportunities and access to social structures, education, career progression, status and economic stability and attainment.

Many white people do not feel they belong to a racial group or recognise any significance in being white – they perceive themselves as the norm. They maintain the normativity and invisibility of whiteness and white privilege: 'They may minimise the significance of race given their investment in loving the "British Dream" in a colour-blind society' (Wijēyessinghe and Jackson 2001, p.223).

There are different degrees of willingness or interest when it comes to examining certain identities. The identities that are more salient to us are the ones we may wish to explore and invest our time and our energy in. BAME individuals may resist examining their identities when they are in the dominant group, or where they are privileged in terms of class or education. They may feel this diminishes their identification with their race and minimises the acknowledgement of the history of discrimination that they have faced for much of their lives.

So, why worry about identity when we are all just human beings and when race just isn't a modern-day issue? The British Social Attitudes Survey (NatCen 2017) tells another story and sets the context.

In the 30 years between 1983, when the National Centre (NatCen) for British Social Attitudes Survey was founded, and 2013, when we last asked the question: 'How would you describe yourself…prejudiced or not prejudiced against people of other races?', the proportion of the public who described themselves as either 'very' or 'a little' prejudiced varied between a quarter and over a third of the population. It has never fallen below 25 per cent. Most significantly, when it comes to racial prejudice, we are not seeing the clear trends towards social 'liberalisation' that are so marked in other areas, particularly attitudes to same-sex relationships.

The 2014 European Social Survey (Kelley *et al.* 2017) asked some questions about race that shed light on this area. When asked whether 'some races or ethnic groups are born less intelligent', 18 per cent of UK respondents said yes. While a clear majority rejected this idea, a substantial proportion of the public holds a view that indicates a significant racial prejudice. The report concludes:

> Inequalities associated with race are endemic in UK society, across income, education, work, health and criminal justice. Public debate often focusses on extreme or more overt forms of racism expressed by individuals, such as hate crimes, or the more distant, impersonal concept of institutional racism. In this context, it is perhaps important also to consider that the cultures and practices of our public and private institutions are made by individual people, and that even subtle prejudices can lead to significant inequalities. (Kelley *et al.* 2017, p.12)

What next (making personal choices)?

In relation to a white majority environment, we need to be compassionate towards ourselves in a way that does not involve evaluating how good or worthy we are. Liberating ourselves from thoughts and feelings that are imposed on us takes time and during this process we need to be caring and supportive towards ourselves. Learning from your own direct experience rather than being heavily reliant on the rules learned from other people tends to lead to a more flexible and adaptive resilient outlook (Robertson 2012) – for example, adopting the role of a kind friend, reading or thinking about common experiences we have with other BAME people, discovering shared emotions and experiences that remind us we are not alone but are a part of a huge diverse world.

Treating yourself like a good friend and seeing what happens

This adapted exercise can be done as a stand-alone exercise or in 'the moment' when you notice critical thoughts or harsh self-judgements you hold about yourself.

EXERCISE: How would you treat a friend?

Being a bit tough on yourself when you need to self-motivate or stop procrastinating is not necessarily a bad thing, but if you have a tendency to talk yourself down or beat yourself up regularly, it may be a sign that you have got into a pattern or habit of beating yourself up that serves only to compound feelings of low self-worth and lack of self-compassion.

By reflecting on how you are with people you love and care about, i.e. a friend, close relative or child who is upset or asking for your help, notice how you respond to them and what you say and do to help them feel better.

- Compare this interaction to how you respond to yourself when you are feeling vulnerable or upset. What are the differences and why?

- How might you respond differently to yourself? What might you say to your scared self or the self that fails? How might you help to raise her even when she falls? What words and tone would be more allowing and less harsh?

- With practice it will be possible to nurture the seeds of self-compassion. Even small shifts such as finding humour in your failings or allowing yourself to learn from mistakes, can make a big difference over time.

- Write down all the things that make a good friendship and then reflect how you can turn this around onto yourself – how you can be that good friend to yourself.

Neff and Germer (2018) introduce three core components that will help you to grow compassion for yourself and others. This can help if you are unnecessarily hard on yourself or need to take extra care of yourself during a difficult time.

The first is *Mindfulness*, which can be described as the process of bringing active awareness to your emotions. In doing so through writing or reflecting, try to be accepting and non-judgemental, as this allows acknowledgement of feelings that we might usually suppress due to shame, fear or denial and spend vast amounts of energy battling with. By practising a neutral non-attachment flow to thoughts, feelings and physical sensations, you can create space between yourself and your judgement. You enter into self-observation that does not have to be labelled with your own or others' critical stances.

The second element is *Common Humanity* and how being human is being imperfect, and painful experiences are part of living in a world that is unpredictable, messy and contradictory. We all feel pain, hopelessness and loss at some point in our life and acknowledging that there are others experiencing exactly what you are having to deal with can help you to feel less alone in the world when life is really challenging. Other people's stories where there is honesty and vulnerability within can help to bring people together to inspire a way forward.

Third, *Self-Kindness* is offering yourself kind words that bring some comfort and understanding, as you would offer to a friend or child. Offering your inner child a gentle approach with a tone that is non-threatening and reassuring can help to restore feelings of safety and resilience and a strong sense of a personal and unique identity.

Keeping a journal is one way of committing these core elements into a daily practice, so that self-observation starts to develop naturally and supports you in your day-to-day life, helping you to make sense of events, people and your own inner voice. You don't have to write reams; just a small reflection with supporting words expressing compassion for yourself is a good start and can help to develop internal clarity, and improve your life and relationships by fostering a new understanding beneath the constant chatter of our minds (Gibbs 1988; Neff and Germer 2018).

As we progress through this book, we will look at the other wellbeing and resilience principles that can support us in creating healthy identities. Wellbeing is not a fix-it solution to life's challenges. It's about encouraging and empowering a positive attitude by increased self-knowledge that accepts multiple aspects and embraces both good and bad qualities. It's about understanding on a fundamental level that you are worth care and attention, even when you doubt yourself or feel minimised in a majority culture arising from the experience of modern racism.

Identity development is a continuous process that may change through different stages of your life and will, without doubt, continue to move and shift. We live in an increasingly globally diverse world where identities will switch and nothing stays the same. History once had the power to name and blame us but now more than ever we can choose to define ourselves. I imagine that will throw up more complexities than we ever imagined, but at least we won't be tied to ones that were once forced on us.

Allowing other people to influence those changes, prevent those changes or deter you from your individual unique journey, through what is still a complex and a racialised landscape, will stop you from securing a confident sense of your wellbeing.

Engaging in doubts or judgements about your identity can reduce your confidence. Developing, accepting and maintaining a positive attitude towards yourself while managing the impact of everyday racism could present an ongoing challenge.

However, developing and growing within the limits of the context, culture and community will support and enhance your wellbeing. Making steady progress and taking the smallest of steps can make a real and lasting change and impact on your daily life.

Chapter 2

ENVIRONMENTAL MASTERY

◔ *High environmental mastery:* You have a sense of mastery and competence in managing the environment, control a complex array of external activities, make effective use of surrounding opportunities and are able to choose or create contexts suitable to your personal needs and values.

◔ *Low environmental mastery:* You have difficulty managing everyday affairs, feel unable to change or improve surrounding contexts, are unaware of surrounding opportunities, and lack a sense of control over the external world.

Understanding your environment

This chapter is about your individual experience and not about a prescribed experience or some hand-me-down experience that does not suit you. How you experience your environment is unique and individual. I hope this section will support you in reflecting on this distinctiveness rather than informing and advising you of your understanding of your world.

The experience of not feeling at home in your environment, feeling ill at ease or even scared can lead to a constant state of stress and anxiety for some BAME individuals. You may have experienced all kinds of discrimination, ranging from microaggressions, which we will examine further on, to verbal assault or even physical assault. Racism is unfortunately persistent and makes for an unfriendly, unpredictable and cruel companion.

Many aspects of our lives are, to some extent, affected by the different environments we inhabit. If we were to paint a picture of the environments we occupy, the painting would illustrate the spaces in which we work, live, travel, learn and the communities that surround us. Having some semblance of choice and control over our environment can help us to feel grounded and competent in mastering it, with the aim of making sure it meets our personal needs and values. Managing these environments is a challenge to say the least. For example, in workplace environments, our time, purpose and energy are directed to the aims of the work in hand even though the work culture may have been fashioned (unconsciously or not) to meet the needs and extend opportunities of the dominant demographic that is white. Walking the tightrope above the dominant culture demands a balancing act – holding steady while negotiating racism in all its forms and expressions. It is no simple challenge.

Feeling overlooked, excluded or having to work twice as hard to progress can take its toll on your wellbeing. How do you feel about your worth when your environment systematically communicates different messages of worth and treatment? The power of the 'social context' to shape a person's identity, self-esteem, values, beliefs, behaviours and perceptions is wide-ranging.

Our environment can be a tough one to navigate, and everyday racism with its covert and sometimes indirect and subtle elements can and does impact on the daily lives of many BAME people. The impact of feeling excluded can have an emotionally damaging effect on wellbeing. We are living in the territories of difference where racism writes and delivers its narratives, forever creating distance-denying similarity and sending out messages that we don't belong. We need the skills and knowledge not only to protect ourselves but also to learn to grow and heal in response to racism, otherwise we are merely hostages to something we are unlikely to change within our lifetimes.

In *The Fateful Triangle,* Stuart Hall (2017) refers to race as 'one of those major or master concepts that organise the great classificatory systems of difference that operate in human societies' and that this classificatory system has a 'powerful a hold on the human imagination' (p.33). For this reason, it is essential we learn to develop a range of strategies and responses that will go some way in gaining a sense of mastery over the environment, regardless of and despite its powerful classificatory systems. It seems to me that exploring and increasing your knowledge about your environment is a first step towards understanding it. For instance, below are examples of words that describe either supportive or unsupportive environments. Being able to recognise what type of environment you are in will enable you to make changes, however small, because of the increased awareness, understanding and information you have gathered.

Figure 2.1: Supportive and unsupportive environments

It is worth spending time reflecting on Figure 2.1. This may be the first time you have thought of your environment in this way. Bringing into consciousness what has remained unconscious is a step forward in a direction of travel that will help you to envisage the possibility of change. If you do not recognise that you are in an unsupportive work, school or community environment, how can you even consider making any of the necessary changes that will increase the opportunities that surround you? The very first step involves recognition and awareness of your current circumstances. Most people have a vague and fuzzy sense that things are not right. Fuzzy feelings are not enough to help you find the pathway to a clearer understanding. Putting the vagueness into words and naming your experience is key to the process of change. The goal of this reflection here is to help you name the experience and therefore connect to different viewpoints.

REFLECTION POINTS

○ How do you feel you fit into your current environment?

○ What do you do with the part of you that does not 'fit in' to this environment?

○ What are your experiences of racism within the different environments you inhabit, and do you feel supported?

○ Who are you when you are not being judged for being different?

○ If you had more control, who and how would you like to be?

So, how do we manage the multiple environments we live within? How do we come to terms with sometimes lacking a sense of belonging in terms of our schools, our towns and cities and the places where we work and live? Managing complex environments involves adapting. How we adapt and whether the adapations are sucessful or unsuccessful depend on who we are and what we experience. The experience of discrimination can result in fear, mistrust, ambivalence, alienation, loss, disconnection, over-defensiveness, over-assertion, denial and repression. We need to build safe structures that will support the survival of race-based discrimination.

Facing such threats to wellbeing can undermine the ability to master the environment, let alone to feel comfortable, contented and free. It may also endanger the physical and psychological sense of saftey that is crucial to being at ease in the world.

If these threats, micro or macro, are everyday experiences, then how can we maintain our wellbeing when faced with unpredictable enviroments? We can make a start by increasing our understanding and knowledge of the realities we will sometimes face.

Developing a resilient approach to managing your environment is paradoxically also about figuring out what you can and can't control. The core components of adopting a more resilient approach to life, particularly with external stressors, is the understanding that not everything is within your control and therefore giving it too much energy and attention can increase anxiety and trigger feelings of hopelesness (Robertson 2012).

Here we will look at safeguarding your mental wellness so that you can meet life's challenges without burning out and, more importantly, not always giving racism a front seat in your life.

Surviving and thriving in work

Environmental mastery asks us to seek out opportunities to take control of what we can. Unlike our personal space, where we can be ourselves and create a home that reflects our personality and desire for comfort, safety and security, the public realm of our workplace or place of learning is mostly outside of our direct control. Fortunately, there are things you can do to build for yourself a healthier work environment in small ways. Making broad sweeping changes like moving home or getting a new job may feel like an impossibility. Acknowledging this stuckness is a first step to making your feelings concious; bringing them to the surface allows you to view them as they are and to consider how you might make the decision to change. Change might represent the smallest of shifting points in your life where perhaps you begin to gain the support of someone to validate and humanise your experiences of everyday racism. Linking up with other people allows you to have new conversations and opens the door on new possibilities previously disregarded.

The experience of racism in the workplace

Strict workplace hierarchies are often harmful to people and can become places where we struggle for equality of opportunity. Factors affecting workplace stress include an inability to control the workload, being subjected to dehumanising management styles, a low sense of personal achievement, little social interaction, bad planning and a whole host of other factors beyond our control. In addition, managing workplace discrimination at both an institutional and personal level takes its toll. It may often feel as if this dysfunction is somehow within you; we are much better off locating it as belonging to the organisation.

We may prefer to believe that the workplace is a neutral place as well as an understanding and inclusive place, but in general those are not the findings of current research into these areas. 'The evidence demonstrates inequalities experienced by ethnic minority communities across many areas of life in modern Britain, including education, employment and the criminal justice system. "It is time to acknowledge that many BAME staff do not feel they are operating in a 'level playing field' Diversity, in its broadest sense, needs to be on the agenda at every level in order to demonstrate real and committed action'. Emotional responses to racism are justifiably strong and leave BAME communities and individuals avoiding full engagement and commitment to their work spaces. It is a natural response to find this difficult territory to navigate, even for the strongest and most resilient. When we feel as if we do not fit a workplace environment, we will inevitably reduce our relationship to the organisation in response to the signals it sends us. This is a perfectly natural survival response.

Excluding practices exist within our work spaces, 'out grouping' is standard,[1] and we do not need to say that much about career progression because we know from research that BAME people are under-represented in this area too. Favouritism is rife, because people are simply warmer to people who are more like they are. The manifestations of 'out grouping' are both subtle and overt in the exact instance it occurs. This combination is impossible to challenge because it flows silently through the structures of systems of power so that the existence of unfairness is not easily proven.

The pressure of unfairness and unequal access to workplace privileges can lead to stress-related reactions and depression, having damaging effects on all aspects of wellbeing.

More research is required to understand the impact of misrepresentation, under-representation and discrimination on workplace wellbeing. The crucial point of issue is that if life is such a battle in the workplace, BAME employees who find their feet and their strength will simply move on and, in the words of Simon Wooley (2018), take their 'dynamism elsewhere'. We may no longer wish to sacrifice aspects of ourselves to fit outdated workplaces where hierarchies are not easily questioned, where diversity is ignorantly considered unimportant and where whiteness dominates the discourse.

We know, without doubt, that discrimination and disadvantage are all too often a part of our lived work experience. In March 2018 the government published the 2018 Disparity Report. This audit provides us with a picture of racial inequality in Britain and addresses any remnants of scepticism with indisputable evidence that disparities exist in all areas of UK society.

The first step towards addressing the issue of social injustice in the UK is to be rigorous and robust in the collection of data. *The Race Disparity Audit Summary Findings from the Ethnicity Facts and Figures Website* (Revised March 2018) (Cabinet Office 2017)

---

1   As Allport (1954, p.363) describes: 'A different coloured skin removes the person to some extent from our own circle. We are less likely to consider him an individual, and more likely to think of him only as an out-group member.'

sets out to examine how people of different backgrounds are treated, and covers six domains:

- Crime, justice and the law
- Culture and community
- Education skills and training
- Health
- Housing
- Work, pay and benefits.

The advantage of this approach has been to gather data in one portal, consequently making it accessible and transparent to all. There has been understandable criticism concerning the commissioning of the report from many BAME individuals, and I would go along with many of the concerns regarding the collection of data and the lack of action that has followed in relation to making real, lasting and sustainable change. It is, however, helpful to see the clear link the report has made between education, health and wellbeing outcomes and future social mobility. Whatever the viewpoints, the audit needs to be the beginning of a coordinated, real and robust response from everyone to begin to close these disparities.

The UK is in grave danger of becoming an isolated island and one that people may fear to visit, work, contribute to, or make their home if there continues to be a history of gathering knowledge and doing nothing with that knowledge. It is time to set the foundations for real change; efforts need to be made to ensure that people, regardless of the colour of their skin, will be able to achieve equality in life.

Your work environment

Identification with and affiliation to your working environment is somewhat fundamental. In supportive and accepting environments, there is the capacity to contribute resiliently and to work with flourish. In unsupportive environments, the capacity for work will diminish. The tendency to fall into poor performance levels can happen when the positive regard needed by us all is lacking. The feeling of controlling one's destiny in the workplace to some reasonable extent is an essential component of wellbeing.

For BAME people, controlling one's destiny is not always possible. Richard Brislin and S. Suzan Jane's (1997) work provides us with the concept of derailment where BAME people are frequently derailed just as they are about to make a move. For example, stepping up into a higher position in work might provoke increased microaggressions in an unconscious or conscious attempt to derail that person, as often they are simply not trusted enough within our institutions. They are often denied opportunities that will progress their careers. Derailing concerns itself with the subtle removal of certain people from the pipelines of progression. Other forms of derailing come in the guise of unequal access to:

- training opportunities

- continuing professional development opportunities

- extra responsibilities

- management opportunities

- networking with senior managers

- forms of micro-management styles

- recognition for contributions made

- high-profile work

- time out for career development.

Added to these forms of derailing, but closely connected, is the way in which race-based discrimination can take subtle forms, for example through microaggressions. Microaggression is a term coined by psychiatrist and Harvard University Professor Chester M. Pierce in 1970 (Angelis 2009) to describe insults that are subtle, commonplace daily verbal, behavioural, or environmental indignities, whether intentional or unintentional, and that communicate hostility.

Microaggressions often lie unhidden beneath the surfaces of workplace environments. They are not easy to cope with and sometimes simply letting go of passing comments may be the best option available. Choosing your battles is one way of being savvy and making sure the focus of your work life is on your work and what you would like to achieve rather than engaging in every battle that comes your way. This will only serve to diminish your ability to reach your potential. Microaggressions can feel like tiny paper cuts – not serious in themselves but add another and another and five paper cuts in one week, 20 in a month and so on would have quite an impact on how you feel about the organisation you work for.

I am not recommending becoming a bystander to your encounters with racism, but I am recommending looking at the option of stepping away from the 'heat' and conserving the energy it would take to confront the undigested and uninhibited acts of discrimination that come your way. The act of stepping away from negative social interactions is a perfectly viable and understandable choice to make. We will come back to this in more detail in Chapter 4 on Autonomy.

Creating individual value and meaning is an important element of wellbeing and it is best not to let these be hijacked by the social and often oppressive context in which you live and work. By this I do not mean dismissing the existence of discrimination, but it might help to learn when it feels good to step away and when it feels good to be assertive – both options being acceptable.

Anger and outrage are natural reactions to the experience of unfair and unequal work-related practices. As a consequence of managing these strong emotions, we may become worn out and lack focus and concentration on the jobs we are hired to do, which can contribute to a lowering of our sense of wellbeing and our sense of belonging.

Sense of belonging

> It is well known that employees thrive in workplaces containing good informal social relations with networks of informal ties. Nonetheless this basic need is often unheeded and buried under a cloak of targets, achievements and the abhorent notion that everything we do must be evaluated in order to make it of value. This dedication to the tick box culture demoralises and disconnects workers from a sense of community as well as setting up unhealthy competitive behaviours. (Cousins 2010)

Again, it is worth taking time out to explore how you fit within your organisation because if you feel a lack of a sense of belonging and are working twice as hard to fit in and getting nowhere this can have a damaging impact on your wellbeing. Knowing where you are is the first step in finding out where you want to go.

REFLECTION POINTS

- How do you feel you fit into your organisation?
- Do you feel a sense of belonging within the community you inhabit?
- What support is at your disposal and are you making good use of it?
- Does this support fit in with your values and your levels of hurt and anger or do these feelings belong to someone else?
- Do you need your consciousness raising by someone else's moralising?

◯ Are you able to let go or is this something more serious that needs you to be assertive and to look after and protect yourself?

Racism and discrimination are present in all elements of our society and at all levels. You may experience it differently from other BAME people depending on many variable factors, such as where you live, the type of school you attend, your family background and your sense of belonging.

A sense of belonging: mentorship and networks

Linking in with other BAME colleagues, peers, students or school friends who have travelled a similar path can help with feelings of isolation and help you to navigate all kinds of barriers. It is positive to choose contexts that feel safer and more inclusive.

BAME staff networking groups can:

- provide a group of people who understand your perspectives and can help you care and manage the hurtful effects of discrimination and disadvantage

- share knowledge and information such as finding out about new ideas like reverse mentorship – where an employee connects with a senior manager to raise awareness at an influential level (this is not common practice but is beginning to take seed in organisations that are more progressive)

- provide a BAME mentor for you when you start a new job

- challenge negative sterotypical images of BAME people

- provide peer group support

- highlight BAME professsionalism

- reduce inequality by advocating on behalf of each other and as a group challenging the status quo

- provide a space to tell and retell your story until it runs out of energy

- build your resilience by enabling you to share experiences and find common ground

- support you in moving above and beyond the impact of racism, recovering your sense of self and getting back on track with your unique purpose

- provide role models.

A word about role models

There is a place for role models in the workplace, as they can embody qualities and experiences that chime with your own values, aspirations and personal qualities and provide support along your career path or in your job. This is particularly helpful if they are also mentors or supportive managers and can provide a level of emotional support and a willingness to share their own stories with you. However, society often perceives them as having a predestined path or trajectory that is not the whole picture of the struggles they have travelled. At the same time, this can sometimes represent an institutional desire to present positive role models as a means of controlling the negative experiences of many BAME staff.

Buffering can provide psychological protection!

William E. Cross, Jr (Sullivan and Cross 2016, p.20) describes buffering as 'the process in which one's positive racial identity allows him or her to be psychologically prepared for potential experiences with racial microagressions'. Buffering is performed at the level of the individual; however, BAME individuals have a long history of creating support networks designed to carry out collective buffering, such as building staff networks through religious beliefs, political activism and cultural celebrations.

I would suggest that healthy buffering – finding ways of protecting yourself – comes in many forms as outlined earlier. Many of the hints and tips below are about setting boundaries and limits because knowing these can help to support you, guide you and protect you when faced with everyday racism. Colleagues and managers need to know where you stand and what you are not prepared to tolerate, and setting personal boundaries on practical levels will help you to create 'safe buffer zones' that offer sources of protection.

Physical space buffer zone

You may not have a choice over the people you work closely with or who you sit alongside. We are often lumped in with people and must make the best of it. There is the wonderful possibility of making good friends with colleagues but also the equal possibility of having to grit your teeth and bear it to get through the day, particularly if you work in environments that are predominantly white. Try some of these strategies:

- Carve out space that is 'yours', whether that be your desk or your locker. This can help you to feel that you have a little bit of control over your environment. How we interact with our environment will change but having some consistency and familiarity, and feeling more in control can foster feelings of calm and mitigate against a lack of personal agency.

- Request a desk assessment if you are not comfortable – a change of seating, lighting, or an ergonomic keyboard could make a big difference to your comfort and productivity.

- Remember the small things like a beautiful writing pen or a comfortable pair of work shoes that you have invested in. These can make you feel good and are small self-investments that also enhance feelings of self-worth.

- Explore your work environment so that you familiarise yourself with parts of the building where you can relax and give yourself a bit of time-out if you need to. We don't always realise that we are depleted until we stop. Taking time out to recharge mentally and physically during your day is a good habit to acquire.

- When applying for a job or relocation, check out the physical environment and where you are more likely to thrive. We all have varying degrees of adaptability; for some people, working in an open-plan office is a deal-breaker; for others, working largely alone or out of the office best suits them. Understanding what works for you environmentally and making compatible decisions in this area is going to help you in the long term. If you use this self-knowledge wisely and navigate your career path, you will prevent the likelihood of working in a space that impacts negatively on your wellbeing.

Workload buffer zone

Organisation is the key to managing a demanding workload and that means adopting a proactive rather than a reactive position. Not everything needs your immediate attention. It is easy to get sucked into the habit of answering emails the moment they drop into your mail box, or feeling that everything requires your attention – before you know it you can start to feel as if you are 'spread too thinly'. Add into this mix that you may feel you have to prove your worth or are judged more harshly than your white colleagues, and before long the workplace can feel exhausting.

Take a moment at the beginning of the week and each morning thereafter to plan your time and build in wellbeing breaks; this is important as you are prioritising yourself amid the busyness of the day. I'm not talking about an hour of yoga or a full body massage – a cup of tea and a chat with a friendly colleague can be enough to boost your wellbeing and buffer you against forms of discrimination. You are also a priority and even if you must schedule in your lunch or remind yourself to clock off, this is a mood-boosting intentional practice that sends a message to you that 'you matter'. Work is one part of your life; it does not define you completely. As the saying goes, work is replaceable, but your life isn't.

The elusive work–life balance zone

In reality, life will throw us all sorts of curve balls. We are challenged to dig deep into our inner resouces to manage periods of ill-health, family issues, unemployment and the habit of taking work home with us, whether that be physcially attending to it, or it occupying precious space in our head. The experience of racism adds another complex element to the mix. As Dinesh Bhugra and Kamaldeep Bhui acknowledge:

> the acts to which BAME people are exposed include explicit prejudicial events or more subtle forms of institutionalized racism, which manifest as repeated experience of failure and a lack of opportunity to find jobs and adopt a healthier lifestyle. Repeated exposure to this must influence the level of trust these groups show in institutional procedures, bad experiences of which must diminish their expectations of care. For this reason, we must learn the art of 'self-care'. (Bhugra and Bhui 2001, p.96)

Accepting the fact that you can't do everything brilliantly, that you can't fight every battle all the time is a good start! As human beings, we are generalists not robots. We may have the potential to turn our hand to anything, but we don't have the time or even the mental or physical energy to do it all, so having a clear understanding of your priorities and where you want to put your energies is key.

How to audit your life

In the wonderful new version of *Slay In Your Lane* it says:

Above all, it's about being honest with yourself and acknowledging when someone has crossed the line, however you chose to react to it. Seek support and a sanity check from your best friend, your friends, family and cheerleaders, because a cut is still a cut, no matter how small. Not all biases are unconscious and that can be a hard pill to swallow. Ultimately, only you can determine what the best course of action is for you. (Adegoke and Uviebinené 2018, p.110)

Undertaking a life audit through the Wheel of Life can help you determine actions you would like to take and provide you with a clearer picture of how you are living and working, what you might want to change and what you might be neglecting.

EXERCISE: The Wheel of Life

This is a simple visual tool that helps you take a snapshot of your life and see where you may be out of balance.

You will need a piece of paper and a pen or pencil and coloured pens if you want to make it more visually impactful.

- Draw a large circle and divide it into ten segments, like a pie.

- On the outer edge of each circle write *Self-image, Career, Finance, Health, Social, Family, Love, Recreation, Contribution and Spirituality.* Feel free to replace or add any of these areas with ones more meaningful to you.

- Along each inner line of the segments write 0–10 from the inner circle outwards, with 0 being the lowest and 10 the highest.

- Now give a rating to each area of your life depending on how you feel you are functioning within it and how satisfied you are. Joining up the ratings will show you clearly, like a graph, where your life satisfaction is lower and where you are experiencing positive life satisfaction and mastery.

Ask yourself some honest questions about what you see and what areas you may want to invest in, such as spending more quality time with your family and less time on social media. Converting the findings into a list or post-it notes and transforming your desire to create balance by setting goals with commitment and conscious application will help you to achieve enhanced wellbeing in many areas of your life.

The key is honesty and a willingness to make changes once you have decided you want to shift the balance. The aim is not to achieve perfect balance in all areas, but certainly the ones that have meaning for you. This is of particular relevance if you find yourself overwhelmed in predominantly all-white working environments, because being committed to yourself in all the different areas of your life is giving the detrimental effects of discrimination less of a chance to take hold over you.

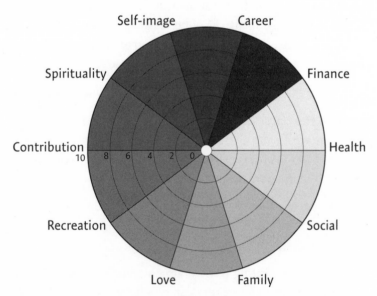

Figure 2.2: My life wheel
Adapted from the Wheel of Life concept© developed by Paul J. Meyer

Technology and agile working

As technology advances and business is increasingly being conducted through social media, it is becoming challenging to maintain boundaries between work and our personal lives. It can feel at times that the boundaries are being blurred to such a degree that we rarely feel 'off-duty'. This is particularly the case with agile and home working, where your place of work might be your sofa, kitchen table or the local coffee shop. The work environment, as with technology, is becoming more fluid and requires us to adapt to a changing landscape.

- If you are home working, home studying or agile working, you can still carry the ethos of productivity into your home environment by setting up a space or corner of your home where you are 'in the office'. Some people work comfortably in front of the TV or need some background noise; for others complete silence is the best environment for them to concentrate. Think about how best you work and when you might need human connection. It can be incredibly isolating and boring to work for long periods on your own without speaking to anyone, so consider in advance how you will make contact with others and build that into your weekly schedule.

- Social media can sap our time and energy with five minutes on Twitter or Instagram magically turning into half an hour. This can be damaging to our productivity and ability to focus on one thing at a time. The result is that we can feel we are not fully present, and the quality of our work and human-to-human interactions can suffer. Take control of this by incorporating a digital detox into your routine to build self-discipline and tackle any compulsive behaviours that may be creeping in around the use of your smartphone.

    - Consider using an app that will track how long you spend on social media apps or the internet so that you are clear on how much time you are living in the virtual world. When you collate the results, consider where some of this time could be spent instead and how much time you would want to spend if you had more control.

– Give yourself an allowance each day to establish a maximum time limit for all your devices. If you currently spend two hours a day on social media, start by cutting that down to one hour a day, and set an alarm on your phone or watch to remind you to check-out. Take stock at the end of the week.

– Be realistic about cutting down. Technology has become our co-pilot in life and supports us in so many ways, to relax, work, maintain friendships…so don't set yourself up for failure by going cold turkey. Establish new habits to engage with tech such as in your lunch break or after dinner, as this will be easier to stick to than trying to eliminate use for the whole day.

– Reduce your reliance incrementally so that you tackle one thing at a time. If you're a boxset binger and this is taking over your weekend, tackle this first before moving on to your smartphone. Give yourself specific targets and commit to changing this habitual behaviour.

– Keep tech out of the bedroom. It can interfere with sleep by disrupting your body's natural wind-down process. Try and switch off at least two hours before bed.

– When with others, think about how tech is dividing your attention. Imagine how much more engaging and fulfilling your relationships will be if you're not checking your phone every five minutes.

– Find a detox buddy or commit to reducing tech time as a family.

–   Challenge yourself to leave your gadgets at home when you go out, maybe at the weekend. If this sounds too drastic, put your phone on silent instead or switch it off during a meal.

–   Tell people what you are doing as this may open up a conversation about tech use and raise awareness about how disruptive it can be if you don't take some control. It can also motivate you to keep going, knowing that you'll be asked how you're doing.

Taking control of your environment to create a space and energy that you can thrive in and be able to meet your wellbeing needs at least some of the time will help you to gain mastery over your work life. If you can create pockets of calm and relaxation and buffer the numerous distractions that modern life brings, you will feel more at peace in yourself, and the quality of your work will reflect this.

Creating supporting structures to enable a sense of wellbeing is essential when the environment presents real barriers to your inclusion. We cannot always control what occurs externally but to some extent we are more able to control what goes on internally, that is, our thoughts, feelings and behaviours. Making sense out of who you are and who you would like to be is an internal process – we cannot side-step what people think of our outward selves.

Below are six key proposals, originally devised to support dialogues between different cultures, drawn from the Unesco Report (2009). These have been adapted by me and my proposal is to demonstrate how they can be used as a personal guide to cross-cultural communications that are encountered in our institutions, communities and wider cultures.

1. Nurture and develop your difference and diversity rather than try to entangle yourself in being like the majority. Find level playing fields where you are able to call attention to these aspects of yourself.

2. Discover your own spiritual, religious and cultural beliefs and once named try to acquire more confidence in bringing

these ideas into your everyday conversations. This is about becoming more creative and authentic in your approach to others, breaking self-imposed boundaries and fostering more complex views of your own and other's worlds.

3. Surround yourself with people who are open, creative and appreciate overlapping cultural identities, and, where possible, minimise bias conversations.

4. Welcome all cultures with equal respect and dignity.

5. Being actively tolerant involves mutual respect. Expect this approach from people in your life. Understand that legislation often makes promises it can't keep in terms of your everyday communications – microaggressions exist and need to be lived through.

6. Develop a language to help people understand your unique and individual diverse lived experience, without doing harm to others – your identity is not fixed, your identity is in the process of becoming. Your perspective of the world deserves attention and understanding.

This list provides some guidance, making it possible to navigate the wider culture with some supportive structures. Gaining knowledge and understanding is the first step to change.

Giving your life purpose and living out that purpose in your everyday life will help you grow towards improved wellbeing. Your beliefs and values are your own and others may approach these with ignorance and trample over them with the blunt instruments of fake knowledge that is held without any thought to the complexity that is you. If we create stereotypes and if we discriminate against others, labelling them with fixed identities, then this will create barriers to having meaningful conversations and relationships with people who are different to ourselves.

The Unesco Report (2009) also proposes that successful intercultural dialogue is not so much about gathering knowledge of others but rather developing the ability to listen and 'wonder'. It goes on to introduce three elements involved in conscious and mindful listening, these are humility (we cannot know everything), hospitality (inviting and engaging with others) and frame of reference (empathy).

Western notions of high and low cultures and of the 'West' and the 'Rest' (Unesco, 2009, p.269) have no place in our modern landscapes. Understanding and accepting our own differences and those of others is emerging as a key concern. If we end up losing sight of our common humanity and seek out conflict as opposed to appreciation and connection, then we will only increase our own and others' alienation, indifference and detachment rather than find deeper meaning and connection to others and have the aim and goal of the betterment of human relationships across the world, and on a micro-level between those we encounter in our daily lives.

Furthermore, we need to reach out and include other experiences, learn to be receptive, listen and ultimately develop the capacity to walk in the shoes of others who tread often ignored and unwritten realities.

In the profoundly moving and must-read book *The Good Immigrant* (Shukla 2016), Vera Chok writes of her unique and individual experience:

> What with the whitewashing of history and the darkness surrounding slavery and oppression, I don't feel as if I own, or am allowed to own, 'real suffering' because of the colour of my skin. Instead, I bear a different kind of badge, one I'm suppose to be pleased about: 'model minority'. Is yellow too pale a colour to shout about? (p.44)

> Powerlessness is a particularly heavy weight to fling off. In order to be attractive to men of any colour, we are expected to be small and pliable. There is an alternative stereotype – the cold, automaton, dominatrix, femme fatale Asian women – but we don't seem to be mail ordering as many of them lot. (p.40)

Managing all of this requires some form of creative intervention, accommodation or adaption. Learning to draw on and to recognise your uniqueness as you journey through such complex terrains will support you in developing your confidence and resilience. Trust yourself, trust your inner voice and most of all trust your instinct – particularly if something feels wrong, then it most probably is.

This is easier said than done; we all need reassurance and if you doubt aspects of your lived experience then reach out and speak to other people who are from BAME communities. Reach out to people whom you trust not to be overly defensive and over-reactive. Don't get drowned out by the experiences of others. The important thing is for you to come to terms and move on from what you have experienced.

Brislin and Cushner (1997) list some of the daily challenges facing BAME individuals that demonstrate strength and resilience in working environments which engender feelings of not being good enough and where we feel we must work twice as hard. They highlight the fact that BAME employees manage to work successfully when in the position of lone worker in predominantly white workforces. They show abilities to adapt and succeed while overcoming disadvantages such as constantly having to be the one who needs to be flexible and make the compromises (Brislin and Cushner 1997). Often BAME staff are placed by default into equality roles because the organisational BAME demographics are so low. For example, often BAME staff are overly encouraged to support equality agendas in organisations without necessarily declaring a particular interest, to suit the organisation.

Below are reflection points to support you in thinking differently and overcoming and developing resilience.

REFLECTION POINTS

G What does overcoming mean to you?

G How has it made you feel, behave and think when you have overcome something in the past?

◌ How would you prefer to feel, behave and think?

◌ Is there someone you could talk this through with and is that person someone who shares your values and beliefs and someone you trust?

◌ What is your contribution to your environment?

Racism in school environments

Sadly, there are many concerns related to childhood development affected by the experience of racism. BAME children face different demands and challenges from those of their counterparts. Aside from these demands and challenges, it's notable that many BAME children discover creative ways of adjusting and adapting to their environments that then allow for normal and healthy development.

Throughout my working life I have counselled many BAME clients who have recounted their experiences of race-based discrimination in its many forms. And what has always struck me is that by overcoming and owning the experience of racism as part of their lived reality this has then contributed in some small way to a positive self-worth and resilience.

It is however important to protect children from racism. 'Preparing children for racist interactions is important because it allows them to attribute the discrimination and bullying to the bully, not to a personal defect within themselves' (Iyer 2013).

Instilling ethnic pride is essential as a means of insulating children from the experience of racism so that they learn to accept what is theirs and what firmly belongs outside of themselves.

A strong sense of self, as well as knowing where to access the best support, will help children emerge out of these experiences relatively unharmed. For BAME children, race-related experiences can be overwhelming and as they grow older and come into more contact with their social environment, they are more likely to encounter the existence of racism. These encounters are likely to trigger an examination of their identity and the painful understanding that they are not as safe as they thought they were.

Discovering you are part of an excluded and less powerful group that faces a myriad of social barriers is undoubtedly painful as well as complex. Racism and discrimination are present in all levels of British society; whether children are schooled in the inner city or outer city suburbs, the colour of their skin is still a marker of oppression (Franklin-Boyd 1989).

Anger and resentment can build on the discovery that one is different and is at times excluded from full participation in the wider culture. Children need to develop a positive racial identification and feel they are accepted within their school environments, where they meet society head on and, like all children, face the difficult task of growing up.

In the book, *Cultural Diversity*, Diller (2007) describes the development of an 'oppositional identity', which rejects characteristics and behaviours seen as white. Oppositional identity serves two functions:

- Protecting and conserving one's identity from the psychological assault of racism.

- Keeping the dominant group at a distance.

- Attachment to the peer group is seen as a positive coping strategy in the face of distress – a stronger sense of determination grown through a 'rite of passage' towards a sense of grounding.

CASE STUDY

Mo is 13. He is becoming aware that he is different as he is at the receiving end of comments related to his skin colour. Subtle microaggressions are becoming part of his everyday life. In order to protect and conserve his identity, he has decided to focus on his art work and he has been told he is very good at painting. He develops and researches Bollywood posters and makes cartoon characters from magazines left around the house by his parents.

He receives a very positive response from his teachers and this, to some extent, protects and conserves an identity that is otherwise receiving messages that he does not quite fit and belong.

Mo chooses to focus on creative and adaptive strategies and strengths that emerge out of his lived experiences. He has adapted an oppositional identity that also increases his resiliency. This involves strengthening personal characteristics, such as the ability to focus and be determined to develop his talent for drawing regardless of what is happening around him. Although the comments do not stop, he does not feel crushed by them, because he is developing an internal strength and as a result he is in the process of forming a buffer against the injustices dealt out to him. However, we need to be mindful that a child like Mo does not use his school work to defend against his treatment in school and become socially isolated as a result.

In school situations, the child who is different may be on the receiving end of negative 'out grouping' behaviours, both from pupils and from teachers. You may receive special privileges (perhaps in the form of receiving patronage), or you may be scapegoated, ostracised, marginalised and excluded, or it may be that your school life is inclusive and free from discrimination:

> One of the most difficult tasks for BAME families, irrespective of socioeconomic level, is educating their children about the realities of racism in this country, while concomitantly teaching them to strive to be 'all that they can be'. This is not an easy task. A parent must help a child to develop a sense of self and give enough information about the realities of the world – so they are prepared without becoming bitter. (Franklin-Boyd 1989, p.25)

Children need a strong emotional base to allow them to cope with race-based experiences in school and the wider community. The struggle for a strong and positive identity is clearly made more difficult by the realities of racism. The need for identification and a sense of belonging is an important emotional issue for everyone, and is undoubtedly fundamental in the lives of children and young people who need a supportive safe environment free from social barriers. They need trusted people to turn to should difficulties arise.

It's difficult to fully convey the impact of racism on a child. Children can be very cruel and hurtful to each other about skin colour and the manifestation of any difference whatsoever. They are often held captive by the colour of their skin and do not have the necessary defences that would set them free. There is no stop sign in front of the word 'bias'. Therefore, in order to survive their race-based encounters, children must learn to reality test what is related to racism and what is not.

If children are to build resiliency, despite being on the receiving end of discrimination, they must:

- develop specific coping and problem-solving skills

- have a history of success in coping with race-related situations

- gain a perception of themselves as capable of controlling their environment

- be able to develop coping strategies under unique circumstances

- use help-seeking strategies – knowing where to go for help

- foster a sense of pride, self-worth and a positive racial identification

- be and stay in touch with traditional networks, community resources and family backgrounds

- find alternative role models

- develop a sense of self that includes their relationship to skin colour

- avoid cultural isolation.

In all our environments, whether it be school, work or the communities in which we live, we should not be left to raise the issue of race ourselves as this would be too much of a responsibility, especially for a child. There need to be clear messages that racism is completely unacceptable and damages all children.

Everyday racism within a school or college environment can take many forms and these may include:

- written or verbal threats or insults

- damage to property, including graffiti

- personal attacks of any kind, including someone being aggressive and violent towards you

- being excluded or made to feel different

- having people make assumptions about you because of your race or culture

- being on the receiving end of jokes

- cyberbullying.

Five ways to deal with racist bullying:

- Accept that it's not your fault – you are not the one who has caused the problem.

- Tell someone what is happening to you.

- Keep some evidence of what's happening, such as a diary of events.

- Try to keep yourself safe – walk home with someone rather than on your own.

- Report racism, if this feels appropriate and you have considered the consequences, the affect and the possible outcomes on your wellbeing.

Family and friends

What if family and friends take the attitude that racism is kind of normal and there to be accepted? As a child, this can be very confusing – your gut feeling is telling you that something is very wrong but the people you love and care about are shrugging this off. This can be an extremely isolating experience leading to the internalisation of feelings that you are not good enough and that you need to be better, stronger and more capable. This can lead on to the development of unhealthy coping strategies, such as developing perfectionist traits, and always working above and beyond to prove to yourself and others that you are good enough.

Becoming mindful of perfectionist traits is the first step to recovery. Taking your foot off the throttle and slowing down to take in a less one-directional viewpoint will open other neglected areas of life. You are, to some extent, in the driving seat and if you are making conscious decisions that benefit your health and wellbeing, you can go as fast or as slow as feels right for you. A conscious choice then becomes a far more viable one.

If you are stereotyped – for example, made to feel you are a good dancer or good at sport or maths – people may have made assumptions about you that bear no relation to who you are. This can feel very uncomfortable but sometimes we make the decision to go along with other people's expectations, just to keep the peace. This is not in itself a negative form of responding – it could be the least damaging approach – but it is worth considering and thinking about who you are in relation to other people's imaginings.

Jokes and banter

Even if there is no intention to be racist, jokes can still hurt. They are difficult to manage and to process, especially if you were a child when this happened. Joking can leave you feeling alone because you are the only one unable to laugh and go along with what is considered lighthearted and fun. If it feels safer to do so, some people laugh alongside their colleagues and peers. My take on this issue is to do what you need to do to survive and adapt in certain environments. Coming up with great responses and witty comebacks is not necessarily that easy, and other people's racism is not your responsibility so you do not need to take ownership of it. Quietly walking away might be all that is needed. However, always put your safety first. It's important not to change the way you feel, think and act to fit in – but it's also important to learn to adapt to your environment if it feels safer to do so. We need to feel at ease with the ways we choose to negotiate society, and the way in which we negotiate jokes and banter must be our decision.

Nobody has the right to call you names or to treat you badly. You should be treated fairly and with respect. Holding on to a sense of your unique self will support your wellbeing and make it possible to make conscious and mindful decisions about how to react – how, when and where you react has to be your choice.

You matter as much as everyone else. But some environments promote silence, denial and misunderstanding. If what has been silenced or denied remains hidden, it is important to acknowledge, as a first step, that other parts of you exist, and find safe spaces to express these. This strenuous level of coping comes at a cost; how do BAME people react to being diverse day after day and year after year in predominantly white work or school environments?

What next? Making personal choices

Thinking about the principles of wellbeing is a significant act of self-care. Show yourself tangible care and attention is of great value, particularly if this has been absent or lacking in your life. Being able to tune into your needs and recognising how you can live a life aligned to your fundamental values will be the supportive scaffolding that you will need.

Discovering who you are when you are not being judged by your environment

If the environment, town, city and streets we inhabit feel threatening and unstable, it can help to learn to build a firm base and from there to build a framework that doesn't have to be put together all at once. In some areas of Japan, a form of bamboo scaffolding is used as it bends in the wind, is flexible, stable and strong and enables growth without restriction and rigidity. In a similar way this concept of flexibility and strength can be nurtured by attending to our wellbeing so that when the winds blow and we experience increased pressure or feelings of loneliness we can respond and fulfil our emotional needs without creating barriers and resistance.

For example, how we respond to stress can influence our physiology and mental health significantly. We can panic or want to run away, but sitting with these sometimes intense feelings and understanding what the situation might be triggering can help process this automatic response and allow for that flexibility to come into play, helping to re-orientate and to think more clearly about a way forward. Like bamboo we need to bend so we don't break.

A framework of support can consist of:

- friends who have shared a similar experience

- significant people in your life who you love and cherish

- work

- hobbies

- making your home environment uniquely yours

- making space in your life for your thoughts and feelings

- nature

- activities such as walking, jogging sport

- community involvement.

The notion of wellbeing can offer you a framework to support yourself physically, emotionally mentally and spiritually so that you can feel good and function well.

Racism and discrimination are the most frequently cited reasons for a lowering of wellbeing among BAME people. A positive sense of wellbeing can be destroyed by exclusion, anxiety, societal aggression and mistrust.

The concept of weathering gives us a great image to keep in mind. Weathering may make us tough and resistant to whatever we are subjected to, but may also cause damage to our wellbeing and can take place over many years to such an extent that we don't notice it occurring.

Where to get support

- Advisory, Conciliation and Arbitration Service (ACAS) – tackling racism in the workplace: www.acas.org.uk/index. aspx?articleid=5771.

- Chartered Institute of Personnel and Development (CIPD): www.cipd.co.uk/news-views/changing-work-views/future-work/thought-pieces/talk-about-race-at-work.

- Citizens Advice Bureau – www.citizensadvice.org.uk/law-and-courts/discrimination/discrimination-because-of-race-religion-or-belief/discrimination-because-of-race/#h-race-discrimination-in-employment-and-training.

- Childline – www.childline.org.uk/info-advice/bullying-abuse-safety/crime-law/racism-racial-bullying.

- NSPCC – www.nspcc.org.uk/preventing-abuse/child-abuse-and-neglect/bullying-and-cyberbullying.

- Place2Be – www.place2be.org.uk/what-we-do/supporting-schools/primary-schools.aspx.

Chapter **3**

POSITIVE RELATIONS WITH OTHERS

◯ *Strong positive relations:* You have warm, satisfying, trusting relationships with others, are concerned about the welfare of others, are capable of strong empathy, affection and intimacy, and understand the give and take of human relationships.

◯ *Weak relations:* You have few close, trusting relationships with others, find it difficult to be warm, open and concerned about others, are isolated and frustrated in interpersonal relationships, and are not willing to make compromises to sustain important ties with others.

Ryff's (1989) principle of 'positive relations with others' encompasses qualities of character that ask us to take into account and respond intuitively to our need for 'others' in order that we too are nourished. There is a reciprocal, flowing quality to her definition of relationship – one that requires a level of emotional investment, a giving of oneself that is committed to developing a bond of trust and openness in our relationships.

Negotiating human relationships is something that undeniably faces us all as members of humanity. For thousands of years we have sought to find ways of both being close to others and taking time out; to remain separate and yet connected. We live in a world where communities are rapidly changing to form other different communities. Perhaps these communities are no better and no worse and yet they are moving forward and ever changing in new directions. We see these new communities resulting from new technologies, social media platforms and online communications. We can join in online communities, such as Mumsnet, Teachers Connect and LGBT Foundation. We are also able to access support through forums and websites such as Facebook and Twitter, which provide opportunities to share experiences and build new networks.

It seems that it is now possible to build meaningful relationships through social media alone, and many people, particularly young people, are building and shaping their relationships in this way. We now have the opportunity of building communities no longer defined by physical locations – villages, cities or towns. We are able to relate to a worldwide community where we can find our own spaces and places to be, although online relationships are still possible containers of race-based encounters. Nonetheless, I would agree with Barak Obama, in his BBC Radio 4 interview with Prince Harry (Turner 2017), when he said it was important for online communities to venture out into the real world and meet in person: 'I think social media is a really powerful tool for people of common interests to convene and get to know each other and connect, but then it is important for them to get offline.'

This chapter will attempt to support you in finding ways of navigating everyday racism in your relationships within the current social context. Sometimes we do not fit in, sometimes we are openly threatened, put down and diminished in increasingly subtle forms. Sometimes we become 'fixed' in people's minds as complainers, troublemakers, radicals and even activists. It is like being told to wear a coat that doesn't fit properly but you cannot take it back to the shop and change it. And you are only wearing the coat to protect you from the cold and rain, not because you are making some kind of point.

Finding the resources to build strong positive relations is an essential coping mechanism.

At times our environments are not safe and not easy to navigate, and we may wish to take ourselves away and isolate ourselves. Therefore, it is of huge importance in our everyday lives that we commit to making choices that increase our access to social environments where we feel safe and valued and where we are can discard the coat that doesn't fit, at least for a while.

Human beings need to maintain a sense of belonging through reliable relationships; otherwise, there is a danger of developing an unhealthy self-reliance. Self-reliance is often born out of frustrations with friendships, family and work colleagues who just don't seem to support or agree with our perspectives when managing the impact of everyday racism. This lived experience can be exhausting, limiting and ultimately unsustainable. We may decide to hide from the world and in doing so isolate and limit our possibilities when we would benefit and grow more within relationships.

We would also benefit from different types of relationships. We need relationships that fit like a favourite old jumper we have had for many many years, that we cannot wait to put on and heave a sigh of relief when we feel at last at ease at the end of the day, comfortable in this skin where pretences disappear and we can be truly ourselves. We need old jumpers to support us and to be supportive of others. If we are truly ourselves, we are more able to be true to others and leave our outward appearances behind. We also need relationships that are not so cosy, such as friends who challenge and stretch us into taking up new interests and meeting new people. And we need friends who make us laugh and friends to take us off to the gym or help us to keep fit.

In his book, *Use Philosophy to Be Happier*, Vernon (2013) takes into account three types of friend based on the philosophy of Aristotle (384–322 BCE):

1. *Useful friends* – They share goodwill because they get something out of the relationship. They do not love each other

for themselves but only in so far as there is some good that they can get from each other. This kind of friendship usually only lasts for the duration of the reciprocation. Think, for example, of a friend you may have worked with – you may have needed one another to do your job but now you have moved jobs you no longer interact with them in a meaningful way.

2. *Fun friends* – These are the people we form friendships with to enjoy life, perhaps a friend you have made via a hobby, someone you have a gossip with, and enjoy nights out with. These friendships are all about feeling good, having a laugh and enjoying the lighter side of life. They can ebb and flow and may not develop into lifelong friendships because they are built on the pursuit of pleasure.

3. *Deep friends* – We might describe these as close or old friends, or even soulmates. Unlike the casual friendships described above, these friendships are based on love and are independent of life's circumstances. That's not to say they last forever, as we can grow out of a friendship; however, these types of friendships are based on the deep relating of one person to another and the essential ingredients of respect, trust and reciprocation. These friendships are most likely to survive a falling out or a crisis in either of the friend's lives. Conversations about race are safer with the people we love and trust.

In considering how important friends are to our wellbeing, to share good times, lean on in bad times, to feel less alone in the world and weave into the story of our lives, it is helpful to reflect on what friendship means to you and your personal style of relating. When we are supported and supportive of others in a way that reflects our values and relationship goals, we build a capacity for resilience that sustains us emotionally (Robertson 2012).

When we encounter others in a positive way, we feel pride, we feel valued, accepted and mutually respected. Your outlook on life, your culture and your religion are respected and valued and you have no need to hide these aspects of yourself.

Very real dilemmas face us when we are constantly living in relation to the experience of everyday racism. Negotiating this is enough to wear us all down. At times, we become the object onto which white people project their 'race thinking'. The ability to bounce back in the face of how other people react to your race and culture is a significant quality of many minority groups, leading to the development of resilience.

Finding ways of living life in a fully functioning and flourishing manner despite the damaging impact of everyday racism is a challenge. We may be singled out, we may be blamed, we may be told we are too angry because we state a point of view. We may become isolated within social and cultural environments where we are the only BAME person working and living.

Within these social settings, we might have to face being singled out for unfavourable and discriminatory treatment and pushed into a state of hypervigilance – a kind of holding oneself together, ready for attack. Many BAME people will relate to the above and many white people will seek to view this as over-sensitivity and paranoia. For me, this does not matter because our lived experience tells us something very different and their lived experience speaks a different language and tells a different story.

Holding oneself together

If we experience the conscious act of 'holding ourselves together' and if we are attached in some manner to this way of being, how do we cope? The bodily sensations that come from absorbing everyday racism can lead to anxiety, depressive symptoms and social isolation. Having a choice and making choices about what to absorb and how to protect yourself is both complex and difficult. But unless you know where you are, you cannot get to where you want to be. The value systems of the majority will exert its pressure and influence on you throughout your life. How do you culturally function within a system that has the potential to wear you down in your everyday experiences?

You are not responsible!

Placing a protective coating around yourself and withdrawing from meaningful contact with people from other cultures is not a healthy way of resolving this difficulty. You cannot help being an outsider. You are not responsible for being perceived as a threat because you are different – you were born into a certain space and place in time. Interacting within this space will inevitably produce stress from time to time – this is a rational response. You may feel mild irritation (a kind of 'here I go again' feeling) or you may feel intensely frustrated, and these are justifiable emotions and reactions that can be worked through. By working through, I mean accepting the feelings of hurt and pain but getting back to your own sense of standing firmly on the ground in your place in history, rebooted and ready to take the next step forward and in the direction in which you wish your life to proceed.

To thrive we need to hold on to our resources of resilience, self-determination, optimism and supportive relationships. We also need to be involved in community and it goes without saying that we must learn to lead healthy lives and to have a reasonable standard of living.

Relationships are profoundly influenced by culture, values, belief systems, rituals and traditions. We must accept we are all different – the differences can be vast and the task of finding our feet among this is a complicated one. To navigate this process while remaining authentic – being true to ourselves and maintaining our wellbeing – is a tough path to tread.

An authentic sense of self needs to be grounded in your social reality. You may develop and change in relation to your culture or family background and this can cause tension, but it is also a process of growing and separating. You may need to redefine your relationship to your family, friends, peers, work colleagues or the community you live within. You may choose to incorporate from the latter what functions and what works well for you, sits well with you and fits well with you.

The complexities of living with everyday racism are enough to taint the most composed of human personalities, so we need others, we need communities, friends and family to help us withstand a culture that may be less than accepting.

Relationships are your resource, and these may consist of:

- your community

- support systems

- religious and spiritual beliefs

- work

- peers

- organisations

- voluntary work

- neighbours

- friends and family.

Within these realms, some of your social interactions may be patronising, limiting, undermining, overbearing and intrusive. We can choose to retreat but we need to retreat to places and people we trust in order to regain our sense of self and our esteem, to heal, to regroup and stay active and meaningfully functioning in our own world. Again, it is a juggling act. We may under-respond to situations or we may end up over-responding – finding ways of carrying the burden and not becoming a casualty to it is the journey to better wellbeing.

REFLECTION POINTS

C How can you recognise the strength within your own networks?

C What is important to you and what works for you in your networks?

○ How can you be flexible with people but hold on to your sense of self and your boundaries?

○ Can you take control of your world when you need to? Making even the smallest of changes can have the biggest of impacts.

CASE STUDY

Lilly is a black student in her second year of university. She shares a house with several other students. One of the other students puts her down, makes comments about her hair and skin colour and makes jokes about her accent. Lilly is not used to this kind of behaviour because she was brought up in a diverse area of London and had many black friends. She is the only black student on her course and the only black student within her house. Lily talks with her friends from London on a regular basis, some of whom are experiencing similar issues. Lilly decides to take the long-term view by attending student support services to get advice and help. She does not wish to report any of her friend's behaviour, but she would like to find ways of managing her responses. She attends an assertiveness training course and learns some strategies and techniques for standing her ground. She finds that simply saying, 'I feel uncomfortable when you say stuff like that' has reduced the amount of comments and put-downs. She has slowly distanced herself from this person and has made the decision not to live with her in the third year of her studies.

In the above case study, Lilly has held on to her sense of self and her boundaries and has taken control of the situation, making small changes that bring the least disruption to her focus, to her studies and to the enjoyment of her student life. She has made an autonomous choice and acted in accord with her own beliefs.

REFLECTION POINT

G Can you think of other ways in which Lilly could have responded? For example, she could have reported the student to the university and this would have been an equally acceptable response. There is no one way of being black and there is no one way of responding.

Your values and beliefs

Validate your own values – political, cultural and religious. Your culture is more than just a removable layer. Your culture cannot be ignored – it is how you see your world and make meaning of it that is fundamental. If you come from a religious background, it might help to consider the following:

REFLECTION POINT

G How does religion or spirituality find expression in your everyday life?

G How is it a supporting function in your life?

G Have you struggled with it and, if so, can you find others who share a similar struggle?

G Have other people within your religious and spiritual sphere acted as role models for you?

G Have you been in conflict with your family regarding the above and, if so, how have you sought help and support with this?

G Which parts of your family/community culture have you accepted or rejected?

G How can you at least clear the air in your own mind and normalise your experience?

Knowing and analysing your relationships is useful in terms of defining what it is you need or want from them. Are your relationships judgemental, invalidating, threating or prone to making you feel insecure and unsure of yourself? Or do they offer more than they take and are non-judgemental, accepting and validating of your experiences?

In relationships, it's helpful to ask:

Who am I?	Who are you?	Who are we together and how does it feel?
Where do I come from?	Where do you come from?	How do we relate across these differences or similarities?
What have I struggled through?	What have you struggled through?	Are there similarities or differences in how we have coped and worked things out?
What am I most proud of?	What are you most proud of?	Can we celebrate these together?
What do I have in common with you?	What do they have in common with you?	What do we share?

Developing healthy sustainable functioning and caring relationships is hugely important to our wellbeing. But sometimes we may be so keen to stay involved in relationships that are hurting us we shy away from examining them more closely. Spending time on unhealthy relationships is hard work and takes up way too much of our energy and time.

In every instance, human beings have a choice in how they face life situations. However, some environments are simply more toxic than others and the people within them place their own needs much higher than the needs of groups of friends or colleagues. Their way is 'the only way' and being around these dominant personality types can cause you to feel drained, confused and disempowered. Our wellbeing can be affected by overly tolerating such situations and the people who maintain these unhealthy environments.

REFLECTION POINTS

◯ Is your wellbeing affected by:

> » belonging to social groups who bully, lack generosity of spirit and put you down?

> » unsupportive, demanding and critical friends?

◯ What are the effects on you of enduring these behaviours?

◯ What small steps could you make to meet your needs in these situations?

◯ What changes could you make to move on from relationships that are harming you?

◯ Is it possible for you to talk through these issues with a parent, trusted friend or a counsellor?

Those choices must be made within the situation and circumstances in which you live, and these might be full of uncertainties and limitations. Passively accepting culturally prescribed roles that deny us our freedom of expression may feel the most comfortable option, but it can place us in a position of inauthenticity and lead us to become out of touch with what we think, feel and value. Departing from the inauthentic does not necessarily mean rejecting society and living in solitude. One can feel authentic as an individual and feel a genuine sense of community.

Learning to connect well with others is essential to our wellbeing, ensuring our relationships are about giving as well as receiving. In accepting environments, individuals can function and enjoy their lives. Conversely in unaccepting environments, the capacity for positive functioning and enjoyment is significantly diminished. If a person is making constant personal comments about your skin colour or your hair, there is something wrong. This person is feeling a sense of entitlement and is also feeling able to somehow invade your personal space by making personal comments they would not necessarily make towards white people. This has been termed 'othering'– you become mentally ranked in somebody else's mind as 'not one of us'. This is a common process, and be it conscious or unconscious, the result is the same. It eats away at our sense of ease, our wellbeing and our confidence.

One size does not fit all

I cannot rigidly apply my set of experiences to yours; the aim of this chapter is to offer people different options towards the same goal, that of improving your wellbeing. We must recognise individual and collective differences and uniqueness as well as shared experiences, and include the social and political landscape we inhabit. We are hugely diverse in character, lifestyles, culture, socio-economic status, education, religion, age, gender and so on. There is no one-size-fits-all answer because the contexts in which we live are as unique as we are.

In my view, and borne out by my experience and others I have worked with, it helps to manage relationships effectively if you:

- manage the ups and downs of relationships in ways that are not destructive

- accept that modern racism will impact on some of your relationships and decide constructively how you will respond

- challenge and transform relationships when necessary

- learn to step away from as opposed to challenge, if that is what is needed

- learn to keep your own counsel if it feels right for you

- broaden your world view

- increase your ability to think creatively

- build self-confidence in small ways with everyday projects that focus your mind and your practical life

- understand and be understood in your social context

- involve yourself in a range of social networks

- directly challenge and walk away from people who harm you – and do this with support of friends.

The contradictions

How do we make sense of other people's behaviours towards us and how do we manage what is unacceptable and what is acceptable? So, for example would it be worth saving a friendship because 95 per cent of this person genuinely makes for a great friend, or are you tolerating too much? Is the job worthwhile and worth saving because you value the work and your colleagues above and beyond the odd comment, or is it a toxic place where you have no chance of thriving? Added to this, if we have a pattern of survival and cling to relationships that are harmful because we felt hurt as children and our 'need' for people to be our friends grew too strong, then we must learn the tools of letting go. Letting go is much easier if you can make new friends or have honed your skills enough to find new jobs, or you have ways of coping that involve staying but learning to be more assertive.

And yet we must trust some people, otherwise our lives will be restricted – nonetheless, if we open up too much we can become victims of what other people consider normal behaviour.

> The matter of colour, quiet as it is kept, is still an issue concerning us. Colour still affects our thoughts, attitudes and perceptions about beauty and intelligence, about worth and self-esteem. Yet if we are to stand together and survive as people, we cannot allow colour to become the wedge that destroys us. (Walker 1982, p.67)

BAME people are highly visibile – their mere presence may invoke fear and mistrust, curiosity and unwelcome attention. Helping each other out, sharing and supporting are central to a protected life. Adaptability is a source of strength; flexibility is a means of survival. Modern everyday racism can lead us to fear, distrust, avoidance and anger and we need safe spaces to take these troubled feelings and thoughts, so we can choose how to respond from a place of balance and security.

We all have the capacity and the ability to expect and hold on to good supportive relationships within the context we find ourselves in and even if this seems like a mountain to climb, it is worthwhile engaging, maintaining and building good solid life-affirming and equal relationships.

More on microaggressions within relationships

We have outlined the subtle forms of race-based microaggressions that encapsulate many forms of attack. All too often, white people communicate their anger towards communities of colour through destructive means. Margot Sunderland in *Draw on Your Relationships* (2008) names some of the most lethal of these microaggressions, some covert and some overt, and lists the different forms of attack common to significant relationships. These include put-downs, fault-finding, controlling behaviours, passive aggression, cold silences, blaming, shaming and humiliating. I would add to this 'questioning', and I'm sure many BAME people have experienced the kind of invasion of privacy that comes with this. While 'questioning' may feel as if it is a show of interest, it can be a constant invasion of privacy and personal boundaries. There is an almost unseen powering over by the majority culture that is an everyday occurrence for many BAME people whose lives are lived in the glare of white spaces.

Throughout my life and in particular when I have been able to talk freely and be listened to without contradiction, denial or blame, I have found white allies whom I have been able to trust.

I can trust that they understand and recognise racism in all its forms, particularly when modern racism plays itself out in liberal contexts and among friends. I do not expert them to be perfect as I am not perfect myself. However, I do recognise that white people have an important role to play in challenging oppression and creating alternatives. Throughout history, there have always been people from the majority groups who have used their power to actively fight against systems of oppression – allies are white people who actively work to eliminate racism. They may be motivated by self-interest in ending racism, a sense of moral obligation, or a commitment to foster a sense of social justice and a turning away from the status quo, as opposed to the patronising agenda of 'wanting to help'. Below are the following characteristics white allies tend to exhibit.

- Acknowledging the privilege they receive as a member of the majority group.

- Listening to and believing the experiences of marginalised group members without diminishing, dismissing, normalising or making their experience invisible.

- Willing to take risks, try new behaviours and act in spite of their own fear and resistance from others.

- Being humble – not acting as an expert towards the marginalised group culture.

- Willing to be confronted about a behaviour and attitude and consider change.

- Taking a stand against oppression even when no marginalised person is present.

- Believing they can make a difference by acting and speaking out against social injustice.

- Knowing how to activate support from other allies, working to understand their privilege, and not burdening the marginalised group to provide continual education.

Racism is out there; those days have not gone away and it has not disappeared. This remains a challenge to the BAME experience because sometimes it might feel more comfortable to turn away and reduce contact with people and to shut ourselves away. This might be a reasonable response to feeling stereotyped, out-grouped and objectified, as all these mechanisms leave little space and energy for developing other areas of life.

Energy can be wasted by trying to fit in too much or toning down aspects of ourselves such as changing hairstyles or making a conscious effort to minimise an accent. Equally, taking on the role of activist can be an energy-draining activity and may even be embraced out of a sense of duty. Holding on to anger and blaming others incorrectly is not going to help keep one's wellbeing intact. Making the choice to be assertive and stand up for respect and dignity is, however, totally justifiable.

We need to find ways of nurturing ourselves and our relationships. Wonderful, kind and supportive people reside everywhere, in every street and not only in a few privileged places (Franklin-Boyd 1989). The system will grind you down and your life may become merely a journey of survival if you go it alone without walking alongside other people. As Mearns and Cooper (2005, p.24) put it, 'Humans seem happier and most alive when they are with others.'

When you are part of a minority there are no hard and fast rules, no single idea that can adequately cover how to navigate relationships. But we all need those reality checks that human connections provide because without them we are in danger of social exclusion and losing touch with reality (Mearns and Cooper 2005).

What can you do when you feel excluded?

It can be incredibly painful when we feel excluded; feelings of sadness, rejection and puzzlement can dominate our emotions and have a negative impact on our wellbeing and self-worth. The reasons behind exclusion are doubtless numerous and sometimes it is impossible to know what underlies this situation. In adulthood, we can rationalise why this may be the case: perhaps I wasn't engaged enough, I'm blowing it out of proportion or I've had too much on my plate to get out in the world lately. This is perfectly sensible and may be the case; however, for some people, it can trigger feelings of exclusion that stem from childhood and adolescence and that, despite us growing older and wiser, can resurface when we feel low, reactivating feelings of being unwanted and unworthy.

As adults, we consciously and unconsciously exclude and are excluded. When we organise an evening out with friends and inadvertently miss someone out, or when we do not get that invitation to a wedding that we were anticipating, it has the potential to provoke in us a sense of shame and lack of connectedness.

Think about a time that you were excluded – what comes to mind for you and how did it make you feel?

Now think of a time when you excluded someone. What was behind this and how did it make you feel? How do you think the other person felt?

You may come up with words such as 'lonely', 'unwanted', 'thoughtless', 'mean-spirited'. It may also be the case that you look inwards to try to find the source of your exclusion – that somehow it resides solely in you. Unfortunately, it seems that exclusionary behaviour is systemic within our personal and social lives, so how do we recover from exclusion and how can we learn to be more inclusive ourselves?

Seek out people who share your interests or who have interests you want to engage with. Joining a group of like-minded people with already established common ground can help you feel part of a shared purpose or goal.

In the workplace, look beyond your immediate colleagues and find out who else you could connect with in your organisation, either through working alongside them, on a secondment to another department or as part of an in-work social group. The more people you know, the more opportunities there will be to feel connected.

If you have deep-seated feelings of exclusion that surface frequently, even at the slightest indicator of not feeling as if you belong, accompanied by shame or rejection, consider seeking counselling or professional support. A counsellor can help you to work through strong feelings or barriers that may be getting in the way of forming and sustaining new relationships. This is particularly the case if you have experienced trauma or abuse that is unresolved.

Take a chance and consider reaching out to the people or the person you feel you have been excluded by (if this feels safe). It may be the case that they did not intend to exclude you. Either way, from their response you will get a sense of whether this was the case and can decide accordingly if you want to pursue this further.

Widen your horizons. If you are stuck in a friendship rut with the same pattern repeating itself, ask yourself if it's worth the hassle. It may be time to move on from this relationship or group.

In a work scenario, initiate inclusivity by bringing in food to share or organising a night out or a charity event. If you model inclusivity, then the chances are people will follow suit. Inclusivity is a wonderful characteristic and raises the vibration of the friendship or group, whether this be personal or in work. It is a vital ingredient for positive morale and can foster feelings of belonging, even in small ways such as making a round of coffees and teas or asking if anyone wants anything from the shop.

If the exclusion is more serious, designed to make you or another person feel bad or to push you out of a job, then this is bullying. There should be no place for bullying in a civilised society and it is not for you to take the brunt of a dysfunctional workplace. Consider reporting it or talking it through with a trusted member of the team so that you can formulate a plan of action or it can be handled on your behalf. If necessary, take it beyond the organisation and seek professional/legal guidance. Unfortunately, exclusionary behaviour can reside on the passive-aggressive end of the bullying spectrum and is not always obvious to bystanders, so you may have to keep a log or diary to build a picture of what is happening. It may also be worth considering leaving or having an exit plan if the environment is toxic. It's not worth the sacrifice to your wellbeing.

Scapegoating – the act of blaming a person for the ills of a family or group – is in some ways closely related to exclusion. It is far easier for a dysfunctional or low morale group/team to apportion blame to one person than to face up to their own part in a difficult situation. Again, this is a form of bullying and can have serious consequences on the individual who is targeted, and you should consider seeking robust support rather than trying to deal with it alone (Baumgarte 2016; Vernon 2013).

In his book, *The Nature of Prejudice*, Gordon Allport suggests that maintaining 'acquaintance' with BAME individuals reduces the impact of prejudice. As BAME individuals we probably all have experiences of friendships with white people who we feel close to over a long period of time but who suddenly – out of the blue – reveal a side to them we have never experienced. They make a mistake, they say something extremely uncomfortable and discriminatory. The question is, what do we say and how do we respond? This kind of unconscious bias is often more upsetting then being shouted at in the street by a stranger, and challenging it in these situations takes time, commitment and effort.

Allport (1954) suggests that prejudice, unless deeply rooted in the character of the personality, may lessen with contact with BAME individuals of equal status and is bound up with common interests and a shared humanity. So in the example above, it may be worthwhile stepping up to the job and challenging your friend.

There are, however, some relationships characterised by confusion, dread, anxiety, hostility, indifference and pain. Walking away from these kinds of relationships is often the better option. For white people who are willing to meet us more than halfway, it might be worth considering leaving the door ajar. It seems to me that when we're trying to build or sustain relationships, we need to find our own voices and to some extent our rights expressed through honest communication. We can do this by acknowledging and communicating our expectations to build resilient authentic relationships (Robertson 2012).

The tolerant personality

Allport also proposes the idea of the 'tolerant personality' (1954, p.425) and goes on to suggest 'developing a warmer greater tolerance' where people bring with them friendly and trustful attitudes that enable them to be closer to people regardless of the groups to which they belong.

Unfortunately, there seems to be a public interest in the promotion of negative and hostile relationships; and social media, with its competitiveness and constant judgements, leaves little space for talk and the dissemination of 'warm tolerance' (Allport 1954, p.425). The key components of environments where tolerance exists are places and spaces that are welcoming, accepting rather than harsh and unpredictable – spaces where you do not have to guard against the whims and vagaries of racism.

Find safe and secure bases where your relationships are non-threatening, where your demands on the relationships are balanced by reciprocity.

Allport suggests that 'warmly tolerant' individuals (sometimes referred to as 'peaceful democrats'):

- are assertive

- have a keen sense of fairness and justice

- support the rights of others

- do not hold rigid views

- are less harsh with the errors people make

- make good companions and find fun and laughter in their everyday lives

- show more resilience in the face of adversity

- feel safe to say, 'I don't know'

- are critical of the status quo

- believe in progressive social change

- delight in cultural differences

- can positively value difference and diversity with goodwill and good intentions.

Less tolerant people are likely to:

- suggest there is only one right way – which is normally their way

- be unable to think about 'shades of grey' or the 'middle ground'

- make broad and general categorisations

- approve of the status quo and not want change

- categorise people to make themselves feel safe and as if they belong

- demonstrate irrational hostility towards groups of individuals and attribute exaggerated and overgeneralised traits

- hide behind a liberalism that screens off rigid narrow views held just below the surface.

If these behaviours are directed at you, they are likely to make you feel hurt and possibly remind you of many painful experiences from the past. Keeping an eye out for ourselves is no easy matter and neither is looking after our wellbeing within a hostile landscape, developing 'social intelligence' (Allport 1954, p.429) and social sensitivity and being able to size a person up correctly, comprehending accurately intolerant cues and side-stepping these harmful and uncomfortable relationships. Dealing with others involves trusting your instincts, sizing up people and letting go. Learning to hold on to potentially enriching relationships and walking away from unsafe discriminatory ones is a lifelong skill to hone over long periods of time.

Realistic perception endows us with the ability to avoid friction and to conduct successful relationships while we inhabit the landscapes of 'modern everyday racism'.

It is vital to develop good, healthy, reciprocal, warm relationships, to build and maintain resilience for when times get tough. There are people who make you feel alive and able to be yourself rather than feeling diminished by microaggressions. But disagreements are bound to exist and if never expressed, the relationships are unlikely to succeed – healthy anger is calm, assertive and quickly resolved and an important part of normal relating.

Concern, kindness, spontaneity, adventure and being a good listener are the kinds of behaviours that are worth inviting into your home.

Perspective taking

Kandola introduces us to the technique of 'perspective taking' and says that human relating involves resorting to automatic thinking rather than processing thoughts. He describes this process as a 'conscious means of encountering other people with the aim of understanding the other person's point of view' (Kandola 2009, p.189).

Using a perspective-taking approach we can learn to empathise with other people and practise honing our ability so we are less overwhelmed by our unconscious bias. Kandola offers us two related parts to perspective taking:

- Individual awareness

- Situational awareness.

The individual utilising this process is able to recognise both the person they are interacting with and the situation they are in – and the relationship between the two (Kandola 2009).

So, in an encounter where, for example, a close friend makes a comment and where something has gone wrong, the individual at the receiving end of the wrong doing would step back and take the situation and context into account as well as the individual involved. The receiver, if they so chose, would recognise and value the contribution of the person rather than focusing on the 'bad behaviour' and immediately resorting to ascribing blame.

Unconscious bias is automatic and almost instinctual, as mentioned previously. We are wired to attach blame as quickly as possible and to go on to reject the human being.

We are equally wired to have a self-serving bias where we overestimate ourselves and favour people who are like us and ignore the value of people we have assigned to the out group. Kandola has provided practical guidance in order to prevent 'hastened decision making, conflict and patronizing behaviours':

> Empathy is something you act upon, not something you own. The having of empathy is tied to the experience of engagement with another real person in a real situation, and can't be generalized into a personal attribute. (Kandola 2009, pp.189–190)

It is a term that defines 'doing and action', involving stepping back and applying yourself in the understanding of another's thoughts, feelings and behaviours, and taking these into account.

Perspective-taking allows us to take another person's point of view without reacting too quickly and falling on our own judgements. We don't need to condemn the other person; we may wish to disagree with their point of view and even disapprove of it but we simply need to stand back and view the behaviour from their perspective.

Kandola does not suggest that perspective-taking is a cure-all. It won't necessarily make you best buddies with the person who reaches across your boundaries by asking to 'touch your hair' or tells you that 'black don't crack' but it does allow you to step back and take stock of a situation, taking into account the many differences and variables in each unique encounter. Maybe this person has had very little contact with the BAME experience both of individuals or their communities. Maybe you feel you have enough respect for them in other ways to walk away from blame.

Managing the affects of 'casual racism' is not an easy task and I am in no way suggesting that it is. Remarks like the ones I have described above can leave the BAME individual very hurt, and how we respond will depend on the levels of tolerance we have built up on a single day. If we feel too much pain, if we have not been able to feel safe, or these comments fall one on top of the other, we may have little fuel left to put energy into a perspective-taking approach.

Where to get support

- Relate – www.relate.org.uk/relationship-help/talk-someone.

- Mental Health Foundation – www.mentalhealth.org.uk/a-to-z/f/friendship-and-mental-health.

Chapter **4**

AUTONOMY

⟳ *High autonomy:* You are self-determining and independent, able to resist social pressures to think and act in certain ways, regulate behaviour from within and evaluate yourself by personal standards.

⟳ *Low autonomy:* You are concerned about the expectations and evaluations of others, rely on judgements of others to make important decisions and conform to social pressures to think and act in certain ways.

Understanding the need for autonomy

Autonomy could be described as an ongoing process of learning how to be true to yourself and as such is a process and not a destination point. When considering autonomy, it helps first to take into account your personal choices and decisions, and then what those choices and decisions are based on, and finally the pressures you may feel in needing to conform to other people's expectations.

Being overly concerned about what other people think and feel, and relying heavily on the approval or judgement of others can be disempowering and create patterns of behaviour that deny our ability to act on our own personal standards. If we look outside ourselves to make us feel better, we are far more likely to reduce our sense of wellbeing. However, the process of building and creating autonomy is ever-changing and developing as we go through life and is very much related to becoming independent, self-reliant and self-evaluating.

How we are true to ourselves as individuals is complex and very significant for BAME people who inhabit a majority white culture. Living alongside this culture and choosing and making sense of our values, dreams and beliefs may be an uncomfortable process, bringing us into conflict with ourselves and with others. However, an increased sense of independence and self-determination will strengthen motivation, creativity and confidence and support you in building a solid sense of self. Too much reliance on the judgements of others will limit your opportunities and leave you on shaky ground.

CASE STUDY

Nisha is 35 and works in a large organisation. She is being pressurised by another BAME colleague to join a newly set up network whose goal it is to support BAME staff within the organisation. Although Nisha acknowledges the importance of this to other BAME staff and understands the forms of institutional racism that exist, she does not wish to become a part of this group. Nisha has many reasons for not wanting to join in and does not want to have to explain herself to her colleague. She ends up telling her friend that she doesn't have the time to attend.

Nisha is involved in volunteering in her local community. She works for an organisation that supports BAME people with disabilities. She finds this work emotionally demanding and is saddened by what she comes across in terms of the struggles for parity for BAME people with disabilities. She would like to keep her workplace free from the effort of challenging inequality.

Although I feel that Nisha might be setting herself an impossible task, I understand the choice she is making and, in this sense, she is reacting autonomously to outside pressure and is showing self-determination.

Low autonomy is formed to some extent by family conditioning and our social contexts. Oppressive systems have harmful and damaging effects on our wellbeing. Generally speaking, we all have to make micro-compromises to keep our relationships healthy, as did Nisha. However, making too many allowances or adjustments for other people will reduce your ability to make your own decisions, and harm your wellbeing.

By and large, we cannot mindlessly go about 'being what we like'. Our worlds are interconnected to many different environments, be they social, familial or organisational. So finding our autonomy means finding a balance between the needs of others and our own needs. We must also recognise that it is safer for some than for others to be autonomous. We cannot leave out issues of power and of economics – for example, some people may not have the financial ability to make choices around educational opportunities. BAME individuals will 'still find themselves entangled in conditions they feel oppressed by. Becoming aware of the possibility of taking direction of one's own life does not automatically lead to ideal conditions' (Mearns and Cooper 2005, p.194).

Even though we can exert a certain amount of free will, there are no quick fixes or magic wands. We live in a post-Brexit climate where racial discrimination is said to be on the rise and generally thought to be legitimised by the consequences of the European Union referendum. We need to be clever and cunning in our attempts to take on personal responsibility and self-determination.

CASE STUDY

Singeta is 17 years old and comes from a lower socio-economic background; her parents have remained separate from mainstream UK culture. She has few connections and does not have the same networks or links that enable her to acquire the same opportunities or gain work experiences through volunteering as her wealthier classmates, who have been able to live rent free at home. It is often who you know not what you know that opens doors. Although she excelled at school, she has had to work in a local supermarket in order to contribute to the family's finances. She simply does not have the same ties to privilege that would allow her the choice to work for free and gain valuable work experience, and therefore this restricts her autonomy and career prospects.

In her book, *Existential Counselling in Practice*, Emmy Van Deurzan-Smith writes: 'It is possible to view these limitations imposed by the human condition as dreadful and depressing circumstances. It is also possible to view them as a given framework, within which it is possible for an individual to be creative' (1988, p.195).

Singeta's life circumstances could change, doors might open for her in ways we cannot imagine – nothing stays the same. Life exposes us to its inevitable limitations, endless dilemmas and adversities, where all we are able to do is act creatively with the ingredients we are given. And some people are given very little.

I hope this chapter will support you in seeking answers and meanings regarding your way of life, discovering who you are and what autonomy means for you. One of the first things you can do is to get to know your own personal definition of autonomy and where in your life you see it thriving and where you feel you are making too many compromises. Is there a person or place that is disproportionately producing feelings of negativity, helplessness and unhappiness? You may not want to do anything about it right now; however, tuning in to your feelings when you experience this happening will assist you in considering how you respond to this compromise and if it is worth it. As Franz Fannon writes: 'For ourselves, and for humanity...we must turn over a new leaf, we must work out new concepts, and try to set a foot a new man' (1961, p.255).

Fanon speaks of doing things differently, stepping out of line, and not being tempted by the norm or allowing the norm to throw us off balance.

Throughout Fanon's work he expresses the particular way in which we cannot help but be defined in the presence of racism. We cannot escape the definition handed down to us through the generations. We react to the history of racism both consciously and unconsciously. We may find we over-respond to stereotypes, we may become stereotypes, or we may reject stereotypes – but what Fanon is suggesting is that we are continuously responding to the manifestation of modern racism. It is within this context that we must find our way to a comfortable level of personal self-determination.

CASE STUDY

Kai has just started at university. He is studying history and has discovered that he is the only BAME student out of 80 students in his cohort. The course leader has asked him if he would appear in next year's brochure advertising the course. Kai immediately feels uncomfortable representing a BAME face to incoming students when he already feels isolated. He also feels unable to say no to the course leader, which surprises him because in school he would have had the ability to stand up for what he believed. He realises this is because his school environment was far more diverse and his peer group would share similar views and actively back him up. Kai knows he is responding to an unchallenged norm, but he feels pressured by the university as he is being told how much they wish to recruit more BAME students. Kai feels he is misrepresenting the demographics to incoming students but is powerless to make an autonomous decision.

Kai is working harder and doing more than his fair share to fit in, but it has come at an emotional cost to his autonomy. His gut reaction that this request is wrong because it misrepresents the demographics of the university is going unheard and unnamed. He feels diminished by the experience. He feels diminished by the experience because he feels he is powerless to take on such a large and hierarchical institution. He also feels his beliefs may be denied and his views met with minimal levels of understanding. It is likely that the university is unable to see this from Kai's perspective, perhaps because they have never considered there is an alternative viewpoint and is in a sense acting unconsciously to what appears to be on the face of it an innocent request.

Resisting social pressure to conform

Autonomous actions increase motivation, confidence, self-esteem and creativity, all of which will increase your sense of wellbeing. Our wellbeing is worth supporting, protecting and nurturing. We need to believe that we are deserving of dignity, respect and equality. Being creative means listening and trusting your instincts and valuing your own thoughts and insights (as demonstrated by the women in the article referenced below).

The Independent carried a welcome and informative article entitled 'The many faces behind the veil' (Akbar 2010). The article describes why some women prefer to wear the hijab and why some make the decision not to do so. This article highlights the importance of independent thinking in a multicultural context where women's experiences of Islam are not uniform.

The hijab is often perceived in binary terms, as either good or bad, while ignoring everything in between. It may be worn out of personal choice or chosen for you because of possible pressures from your family background. You may find yourself accepting certain religious or cultural beliefs and values, or you may feel oppressed and coerced, or you may feel something in between and something more complex and nuanced. There are many ways in which we enact inherited religious beliefs.

Incidentally, whatever our backgrounds, whether they be religious or secular, we are all to some extent making choices about our family backgrounds, values and beliefs – and how much we consciously take from them and how much we decide to discard. Many people in the UK were brought up in Christian backgrounds and made all kinds of decisions regarding their connection or disconnection to these beliefs – by some means we have normalised this process but highlighted and emphasised the struggles within other religious communities.

The Independent article (Akbar 2010) interviewed five British women who made decisions either to wear or not to wear a hijab. Here are some of the reasons why these personal choices were made.

For one woman, 'it was something she really wanted to do' and she went on to say that 'above all, the most offensive suggestion to me is the idea that women who wear a headscarf have no autonomy and that it is not a free choice'.

Another woman described a visit to Pakistan prompting her to adopt wearing the hijab, but when she wore it to school, 'a lot of friends started to ignore me, they thought I was different and not part of their group. I didn't have a lot of friends for a few years, but then I found a different group of girls who I identified with. I got more confident and was able to make friends.'

Alternatively, another woman felt that some women who wear the hijab feel they are somehow morally superior to those who don't and she went on to say that 'for this large group of women who otherwise might not have a strong sense of identity, covering their hair gives them…an obvious identity badge'.

Lastly, a woman said that 'headscarf wearing is on the increase because there is so much pressure on women to keep up with the latest trends and some people want to break away from that. People say the veil is a tool of oppression, but I have found it a tool of empowerment'.

The examples outlined above (Akbar 2010) are all unique perspectives that demonstrate new, complex and nuanced thinking even though the women could not help but be influenced by current social and cultural influences.

Women wear 'headgear' for many reasons, as revealed in the *Independent* article. They demonstrate clear, independent, self-determining actions arising out of their experiences. And I imagine these discoveries arose out of their lived experience of being Muslim in the current UK context.

It's interesting to note that these choices did not arise from family pressure or the Muslim community, but were independent choices. Their decisions arose out of a self-determination to act with modesty in their choice of clothing. They showed a respect for their religious and cultural beliefs, disregarded external pressures that have grown out of Islamophobia and maintained their personal standards (Akbar 2010).

Self-image is currently very important owing to the rise in the uses and abuses of social media where we are encouraged to turn our gaze inward and compare ourselves to other people. In my opinion, the BAME experience results in continuously being at the receiving end of the white gaze; and if we are living out our lives in response to this gaze, then our everyday lives will be affected and possibly cause us to become anxious, depressed or even fearful of going out in public. The way in which we and others experience our bodies is tied up with many things, and one of these is skin tone, which impacts on social functioning, how we are perceived as sexual beings, our emotional wellbeing, and how we present ourselves in our everyday lives. Being objectified by white people in casual interactions is a constant in BAME lives.

How to promote a more positive BAME identity

My personal experience of overcoming and being in continuous contact with everyday forms of race-based experiences has led me to develop my own coping strategies for promoting a more positive identity:

- Recognise what you have overcome in your everyday experience.

- Celebrate your actions taken against adversity and your ability to stand your ground.

- Find people similar to yourself and find points of connection.

- Connect to a collective identity to protect yourself from the experience of being invisible or of having no voice.

- Develop as much personal pride as you are able to.

- Improve your knowledge of the real facts (e.g. knife crime in the UK is not just committed by BAME youth).

- Focus on being equal, competent and worthy.

- Develop your own affirmations from BAME literature.

- Make meaningful connections with white allies whom you trust.

- Broaden a sense of your possible self.

- Anchor yourself by holding on to what you believe and value in your life.

- Be aware of excluding positive personal attributes.

It would be worthwhile building on these examples and adding more of your own to the list.

Living your life in response to racism will inevitably limit your choices and narrowly define your options for personal development. We are all bigger, better and infinitely more complex than the definitions imposed by others. From my perspective, whether we take action or not against race-based discrimination, without doubt, our primary concern should be our wellbeing and safety.

Indeed, there is a bigger picture out there and it's a good idea to take a look at it. You can tie your choice to the compromise, or not, or bring in other options that may allow you to reclaim your autonomy, such as a negotiated compromise. For example, Kai could refuse to appear in the photographs for the university because he feels he is ignoring his personal standards. Alternatively, he might decide that going against his course leader is not worth the hassle, and agree to do the photos but consciously prepare himself to say 'no' the next time he is asked.

Kai might choose to discuss his dilemma with his BAME friends. Talking to like-minded people who show care and concern will enable him to feel a sense of belonging and is a step in the right direction towards standing up for himself next time a round. Majority white environments are hard task-masters and we are all learning on the job.

REFLECTION POINTS

◌ Who benefits from the continuing presence of white standards and norms?

◌ Who loses out?

◌ Whose positions are silent and not present in everyday stories?

When reflecting on the points above it would be useful to find safe spaces with people you trust. Expect these conversations to be difficult because you may be covering new conversational territory. Developing your own uniqueness is also the aim of this reflection. You are equal, but you are different. How you enact that difference must be your choice.

Setting boundaries

There is a commonly held belief that when you respect your personal boundaries others typically will too – you teach people how to treat you. In practice, this is easier said than done. As a BAME person, you may experience stereotypical and pre-formed judgements from non-BAME people about your work ethic, areas of interest and personal qualities, in place of your unique personality. Setting boundaries at work can be risky in some respects because of the potential for upsetting people, particularly those in a senior position, who could have the power to fire you or make life difficult!

In some respects, it's often easier to set boundaries when you first start your job so that you can be clear on the ethos of the company and how it treats its employees, which is often revealed within the pay and conditions of the job, the sickness policy, holiday entitlement and whether there is an employee assistance programme. As a BAME person, you may also want to find out how the company meets its obligations for equal opportunities and read the policy on equality and diversity in the workplace, so that you are in possession of all the information you need, should you need to maintain your boundaries formally.

Tips for managing personal boundaries

- *Know your values* – If it's important for you to leave work on time because of caring responsibilities or to keep stress at bay, then a boundary might be that you are not available for overtime. Being clear on what you value helps to establish where your boundaries need to be.

- *Communication* – If people don't know what your personal boundary is in relation to a request or assumption, then you may have to tell them and explain why. That doesn't mean you have to provide justification or an apology, but clear communication can help to inform others where your line in the sand is drawn. Explanations don't have to be personal – you could do this by being factual and reflecting back via a question to that person. A questioning, curious approach can be a powerful way of understanding the reasons behind the initial request and can also diffuse anxiety in the moment and help you to consider more rationally how you want to respond. You may want to buy yourself some time and suggest that you'll come back to them on that. You can then consider their request in more depth and formulate your response in your own good time.

- *Righting boundary violations* – Immediacy or 'in the moment' responses are considered the most effective way of addressing a boundary violation. Communicating neutrally and without blame that you are not comfortable or in agreement with the person overstepping your boundary has a power within but if you put off responding for weeks you will lose that power. This is not always possible and will depend on the person and the potential fall out; however, if it's something you are not willing to accept, then responding in the moment is more effective.

- *Formalising meetings* – This can be an effective way of managing requests so you have time and space to consider what is being asked rather than being ambushed unawares at your desk or at the coffee machine. Asking for an agenda prior to a meeting sets the tone for a professional interaction, particularly if you feel you are being treated as inferior in some way. Stating how long you are available or when you have to leave sends the message to your colleagues that your time is of value.

In taking care of your boundaries you are also demonstrating that you value your autonomy. It is helpful to visualise your boundaries getting crossed and prepare in advance for how you are going to handle this. Questions to ask yourself could be: Will I respond to a request right away? Will I offer an explanation? Will I deliver a detailed explanation or consider a short 'no, sorry' enough?

With practice and consistency, boundary setting can positively enhance your wellbeing and you will probably gain insight into your own autonomy style across all areas of your life. You will be less likely to be hijacked by an emotional response and you will set the tone for your professional and personal relationships. If someone is continually crossing your boundaries despite knowing what they are, it may be time to evaluate that relationship and consider if this is an individual you can continue to share space with.

It is not a nice feeling to be taken advantage of or treated in a way that the boundary crosser would not like for themselves; however, some people may have a low regard for their own boundaries, or not see boundaries as relevant. The intent behind the boundary violation makes the difference, as it may be accidental or unconscious behaviour (as in the case of Kai's course leader). How you address violations needs to be done in a way that you are comfortable with, even if that means starting on something small in one area of your life, such as responding differently next time something similar happens.

A few ways you can say 'no' and buy yourself time to think

- Let me think about that.
- Here's what will work for me.
- Can I get back to you?
- That doesn't work for me.
- I appreciate you asking but I can't.
- I know that's important but I can't.
- Thanks, but this isn't going to work.
- That isn't doable for me right now.
- Oh, I wish I could!
- I'm going to have to pass on this.
- I don't want to say 'yes' then let you down.
- Not right now, thanks.
- I don't want to say 'no' but I have to.
- It's just not right for me.

Autonomy and social media

There are both positives and negatives around social media interactions, and we can make or break ourselves on websites. It is a wonderful experience when we are understood, recognised and empathised with but painful when we are ignored and diminished by the experience of sharing aspects of ourselves online. It is hard to resist social pressure to conform on social media and it is equally hard to avoid 'disinhibition' regarding how we choose to portray ourselves.

The idea of 'disinhibition' has been described as saying and doing things in cyberspace that you ordinarily would not do in the face-to-face world. People loosen up, feel more uninhibited and express themselves more openly. Invisibility gives people the courage to say things that they otherwise would not. In his excellent article 'Online therapy and support groups' John Suler (1996) suggests that this anonymity is about the power of being able to conceal.

Social media presents a contradiction between the freedom to express and portray oneself and the inauthenticity of much of what and who we are portraying. Developing your own 'online presence' and building a picture that is a true reflection of what is going on in your life is virtually impossible on social media. Some people only share positive, comical or attractive aspects of themselves and can become rigid and stuck in their representations. On top of our own online insecurities, we also have to contend with the response from family, friends, work colleagues and so on, and it becomes clear just how much we have to psychologically contend with. We are therefore continuously challenged to make choices as to how we face our everyday BAME lives on social media, most obviously because how we represent ourselves can and does create unwelcome reactions.

Social media can provide us with great sources of information and knowledge about BAME digital identity. Clearly, social media allows individuals to publicly construct and express who they are or desire to be, so we can therefore project an online racial identity. This may serve as protection or, if disinhibited, it can become problematic.

Below is an example of a BAME person exercising a degree of autonomy in defining their racial identity online.

CASE STUDY

Jamal's online identity is made up of references to BAME music, and African American and Black British political struggles, such as refences to 'Black Lives Matter'. Jamal is clearly projecting an online racial identity, and this is possibly one of the few places where he feels he has a voice, some sense of racial group belonging and solidarity with social activism and social justice.

Jamal is presenting, sharing and promoting certain aspects of himself that represent an element of his true identity. It is possible that the social media platforms he uses are allowing him to construct and express who he is because he feels safer online. Jamal could be experiencing what is known as online disinhibition in that he does not feel restricted in expressing his opinions about his racial identity. Online he is invisible; he has a certain amount of anonymity and may feel that doing or saying anything is more possible than it is in real life. Jamal is also constructing positive representations of BAME people.

Social media platforms clearly allow a BAME person to construct and express who they are or who they desire to be, and are an everyday form of communicating identity. Little has been written about the experience of racial identity on the internet, and who we are online can only represent certain aspects of ourselves. However, maintaining a responsible online presence is a protective factor well worth exploring.

A word about the collective versus the individualistic

It is also worth noting and acknowledging that some cultures are likely to be more collectivist in nature than individualistic. This means that the individual's needs are connected to the collective. Much of what is written around psychology ignores the collective meaning of the community and family, and yet we know for sure the benefits of human connections on wellbeing are hugely significant. We are living in a culturally diverse Britain where there are a great many challenges for everyone and these are not necessarily solved by an individualistic approach borne out by years of Eurocentric thinking around philosophy, social sciences, psychology and politics. Eurocentrism is the technical name for the view of things in which a western European group is at the centre of everything, and all other views are scaled and rated with reference to it. We cannot deal with the enormity of this subject here but it is well worth noting that BAME people are making comments about their history and recognising that it has been predominantly written by people who hold power. When you don't hold the purse strings of power it's not so easy to make self-determining choices and resist social pressures. Our worlds are hugely complex and full of limitations and uncertainties. However individualistic and however collective, we all need respect, connection, support, safety and community alongside an ability to be self-determining.

For example, spaces of learning both in schools and colleges are uncomfortable for most BAME people who are aware of just how distorted their learning will be and just how challenging it will be for them to change the status quo. Some BAME academics are rightly asking the question 'Why is our research about dead old white men?' Students are still experiencing academic cultures that are not inclusive. The powers within these institutions decide what is valuable to study and what is irrelevant; the decision-making processes are not equal, and until they are we will have a one-sided account of history dealt out by the so-called 'pale male'.

Our current society continually reinforces itself as the norm – we normalise our culture and, in that sense, our culture then becomes invisible from within. I have heard it expressed that British people feel they do not have a culture and they are losing their culture – sometimes blaming immigration for this. My own view is that British people have a culture that is not invisible to outsiders – we have, for example, a culture of alcohol consumption, of eating certain types of food, of gardening, of perhaps being less willing to invite people into our homes, of politeness, of making way, of exploring, of not saying what we really mean for fear of offending. Off the top of my head, I can think of many aspects of our culture. It might be that because some aspects of western culture are quite negative, we cease to name it as such and can only name and shame the cultural norms and values of others. It would be well worth considering another perspective on our culture – for example, how do visitors and holiday makers view us? How do they perceive our culture from a distance and what are the stereotypes they create of us? This will then provide us with a more balanced approach to the whole issue of culture.

Conforming under social pressure when necessary (choosing your battles)

It's not workable or bearable to rely on the judgements of others to conform to certain social pressures. We need courage to take the opportunity to be self-directing and enhance our wellbeing. We also need to understand that our autonomy will be restricted in certain contexts. If you work in a non-diverse workplace, your choices to be yourself might be minimal, your sense of belonging minimal, and you may well end up dodging bullets coming from all directions. But you get to decide which bullets to dodge and which bullets to block. You are entitled to choose your battles and dodge bullets to survive. You are entitled to stay quiet and keep your own counsel and you are entitled to tone down or tone up your colour in a metaphorical sense. You do not have to measure up to some kind of activist moralism that is safer for some than for others.

CASE STUDY

Nathan is 16 years old and at school studying his A-levels. His school is predominantly white although he has made some BAME friends. He visits his school counsellor to tell her that he is struggling with his classmates but does not say why. Fortunately, his counsellor is

BAME and enquires as to whether there are any comments being made to him because he is black (this is how Nathan describes himself). Nathan instantly replies and laughs at the same time, saying they call him the N word all the time – but that they are joking. The counsellor points out to Nathan that this is a form of racism. Nathan says he feels that his mates use it because they watch music videos where the word is regularly used by black people. Nathan is clever and aware of the cultural world he inhabits. The counsellor asks him how he feels about it and if it upsets him, and Nathan admits that it does affect him and that he spends time mulling it over in his mind and trying to overcome it by 'understanding' how much his mates are confused.

After quite some time, Nathan admits that this is having an impact on his school work and on his wellbeing. He admits to feeling confused, to adapting to how he feels his friends see him (cool, chilled-out and easy going) and this is not the real him – it is a mask of survival he wears to safeguard himself from constant remarks and keep his relationships intact. The counsellor states very clearly that Nathan can get help and that some of what is going on is against the law and might very possibly be a race hate crime. Nathan states very strongly that he doesn't want to make any kind of complaint or to rock the boat in any way. His parents are very proud of how much he has achieved so far and they would be very upset if they knew what he was facing. When asked how he would like to deal with it, Nathan makes it very clear that he just wants to talk about it, to be heard, to feel he has a voice. The counsellor asks Nathan if he has ever thought of expressing his experience in a different way other than through a complaints process. Nathan says he has a presentation coming up where he might be able to raise some of these issues in a way that would not damage any of his friendships. The counsellor asks if Nathan would like some support and help with the project. Nathan leaves the session smiling and feeling as if his needs have been met. His life has not been turned upside down by someone else's needs to 'fix it' for him. He is excited and empowered about researching and designing his presentation and is thinking of writing about the personal history of Malcolm X.

Conscious conforming may be a necessary form of survival, as illustrated in Nathan's case. Raising your head above the parapet is an obviously risky business. Being autonomous in response to modern racism isn't an easy road to negotiate. There is still little honest dialogue around race in most of our worlds. The culture is so powerfully against other world views. Challenging power and acting autonomously is not always possible.

- It would be worth taking a moment to consider what might have happened to Nathan's life if he had made a formal complaint to the school?

- Think about the impact on Nathan of not making a complaint but producing a presentation that contained some less Eurocentric history?

- What would be the impact on Nathan if he did not return to counselling, did not do the presentation and was left living an inauthentic life – dodging bullets with no one to support him or dodge bullets with him?

I see no easy answers; I might pick one of these routes or find others. The most important issue here is that self-determination and independent thinking and actions are not taken out of Nathan's hands. This is a complex case and highlights the impossible demand between autonomy of the self and maintaining the valuable connections we all need to thrive as human beings. It is the world that needs to change; it is not Nathan's responsibility to live up to impossible external pressures.

Exploring unconscious bias and your ability to be your own decision maker

We all have unconscious core conceptions about people's competence, interests and behaviours. It is when we are under stress, or under the pressure of time that our hidden biases automatically come into play and take over the control of our actions and judgements.

Why do we need to understand unconscious bias?

Once we are aware that it is a natural human instinct to act on thoughts that arise automatically, without thought, consideration or 'perspective taking' (Kandola 2009, p.189), we can take time out to examine these thoughts and to judge whether they are fair and reasonable, biased or non-biased. We are hardwired to differentiate between groups of people.

What can we do about unconscious bias?

Putting people into boxes in order to make ourselves feel safe will not break down barriers and overcome the obstacles of living in a multi-racial society. Challenging unconscious bias takes time, commitment and effort.

There are a number of ways in which we can stretch ourselves into thinking outside the boxes:

- Become aware that unconscious bias exists.

- Remain open to what is new and unfamiliar.

- Increase your knowledge of other groups and go out of your way to communicate and learn from people from these groups.

- Ask 'what if' questions (What if I was living under the same circumstances? How would I feel?).

- Engage in active listening.

- Support each other in noticing bias.

- Slow down your thought processes to allow other thoughts to arise.

- Practise perspective-taking (Kandola 2009).

- Go out of your way to experience new areas of encounter, and engage in genuine dialogue.

Coping with both being autonomous and maintaining connections with people

Here are some positive suggestions for doing it differently:

- Seek out more diverse environments, or work towards leaving less diverse environments that are unhealthy. Make sure you take your own time in making decisions – give yourself permission to make changes at your own pace.

- Consider making where you live a valuable and safe space. Make it as comfortable and acceptable to you as is possible within your circumstances. Allow it to reflect who you are, so that when you return, you return to something that represents the authentic you.

- Define and learn to be clearer about your values, goals and actions, so that whatever other people do you have a clear and sharp view of what you want out of your life.

- Acknowledge that life is often best changed by taking small steps – do things that make you feel good about yourself.

- Don't over-think your response to modern racism – don't allow it to take up too much of your time because it is something you have little control over. Work on what you do have control and influence over. Choose your battles and don't let others choose them for you.

- Find allies and don't challenge the status quo on your own – challenge as a collective. If you go it alone, the system is likely to grind you down and leave you exhausted.

- Focus on valuing what is working well in your life, such as friends, family, good colleagues and good working conditions.

- Join organisations that might support you (BAME networks).

- Do what what feels right for you. There are multiple aspects to your life you can move to the foreground or background if you want. (Maybe modern racism is just annoying background noise that you hope will change one day but you are not going to let it impact on your goals and your life.)

You do not have to attain 'perfection' in these practices. You only need to raise your average level of performance to experience growth and make changes. I'm sure we have all witnessed the most extraordinary changes in people's lives as a result of relatively small improvements. Smaller steps are easier to take, and less intimidating. One small step can easily lead to another, enabling you to cover new ground and strengthen your sense of your own effectiveness.

Your values and beliefs about your life shape your relationships with all others around you. If you build a picture of what it is you want and believe, then it becomes much harder for people to derail you and send you off track from autonomous living.

In many instances, we have choices in how we face life situations. I acknowledge that these choices are limited by a socially constructed world where power structures and inequality exist in such a way as to make it impossible to personally challenge long-standing systems. Taking responsibility for our existence and relationship to the world requires us to become more aware and accountable to ourselves. We need to figure out how to walk in healthy directions, taking pathways that are as authentic as possible without rejecting society. Living without connections, living in solitude or hiding away are not healthy means of coping.

The enactment of microaggressions

We can now give a name to subtle forms of discrimination that happen all too often and for the most part go unchallenged: the word 'microaggression' has enabled us to flag up everyday experiences that were previously left unnamed. It felt as if these small daily transgressions were disregarded mainly because we couldn't give them a name and they remained invisible. Therefore, giving these slights of speech a name means that these casual incidents are easier to manage. Being on the receiving end of race-based microaggressions is like being asked to match up to very different standards. I matched up to those standards and just got on with it. We can get used to these small slights but everyday occurrences add up and have a powerful impact on wellbeing. I always knew in my heart that when these things happened I was somehow experiencing a form of communication that was 'othering' me in these brief everyday exchanges.

Although many people have only recently become aware of this word, it has in fact been around since the 1970s. As Derald Wing Sue (2010) wrote: 'Microaggressions are the everyday verbal, nonverbal, and environmental slights, snubs, or insults, whether intentional or unintentional, which communicate hostile, derogatory, or negative messages to target persons based solely upon their marginalized group membership.'

Some examples of racial microaggressions

- Being searched at airports more often than white people.

- Being the last one to be sat next to on public transport.

- Having your hair or skin regularly touched or people asking to touch it.

- Being told how well you speak English.

- Having other people decide your racial identity.

- Being automatically left out of social events because of preconceived notions you would not attend.

- Being frowned on for not drinking in a drinking culture.

- Being asked where you come from.

- Walking into shops and being immediately followed by store detectives.

Because these incidents are hard to detect, they are often disregarded by the perpetrator and the target. Much of the time people are simply left feeling uncomfortable on both sides. When it's more obvious, these subtle biased attitudes hurt and demean people on a personal or group level.

How to deal with microaggressions

In her article 'How to deal with microaggressions as a black woman', Sharmadean Reid (2018) suggests a two-stage approach involving:

- Receiving the comment, for example 'May I touch your hair?'

- Responding to the comment with 'May I touch your hair?'

This approach involves maintaining a certain level of assertiveness. It takes practice to mirror someone's words and reflect back to them the experience of these small but significant personal invasions of privacy.

Dawn Butler, MP, in the essential read *Slay In Your Lane* (Adegoke and Uviebinené 2018), makes the point that you have to tailor your response to whatever the situation allows; therefore she advocates waiting for the right time and holding your own counsel. (I would add that it's essential if going for a soft or hard challenge that safety should always be a priority in your head.) She goes on to talk about a variety of ways of dealing with micro-aggressions:

- The disruptive challenge – strong forceful challenging likely to provoke a strong response.

- The discreet challenge – a softer approach that might mean walking away or taking time out.

- The engaging and educating challenge – involving and engaging the person in a debate.

- Challenging by recording incidents – incidents can and do add up and become a form of harassment (Adegoke and Uviebinené 2018).

There are some poignant examples of the way in which micro-aggressions are dealt to us in a way that makes it almost impossible to recognise, such is the understated trickery. Consider:

- A white couple with many children is said to have a large family – a BAME family is said to breed like rabbits.

- The middle classes living together constitute suburbs, whereas miners constitute a community and immigrants a ghetto.

- White immigrants to Britain, are said to come in large numbers while BAME people come in hordes and waves.

(adapted from Littlewood and Lipsedge 1982, p.138)

Such instances are all individually trivial but can be cumulatively shattering and general enough to make life feel uncomfortable. If we ignore this uncomfortableness, we are in danger of losing our self-respect and dignity; if we react, we might be accused of over-reacting, being over-sensitive and blowing things out of all proportion (Littlewood and Lipsedge 1982).

Your differences are unique and special, and you carry those unique and special aspects of yourself into many different social settings. In all relationships, we need to balance our own needs and the needs of others. This does not mean you turn a blind eye to the hurtful, painful aspects that modern racism brings to the table but it does mean we have to learn to live creatively within a system that is clearly unfair, biased, and unequal. As I sit here typing this, I have just read the news about Lord Sugar's tweet and his subsequent apology. When describing the Senegal national football team Sugar wrote 'I recognise some of these guys from the beach in Marbella. Multi tasking resourceful chaps' (Butler, 2018). Whether conscious or unconscious throw away comments like this clearly show that stereotyping exists within the highest of places such as one of the bastions of all our public services the BBC. Lord Sugar as mentioned above apologised and I see this as a positive action whether heartfelt or not it sends out a message that stereotyping people in this way is offensive, disinhibited and patronising in the extreme.

Being true to yourself and balancing the needs of others in a majority white society

Looking after yourself and taking care of your needs is not a question of opting out of responsibility for the racism that exists within society. It is not your fault that someone left a package on your doorstep that doesn't belong to you. Or that race-based microaggressions leave you on guard and held to attention by their subtle and crooked ways. It is important to acknowledge what you can control and recognise, and what is outside your control, including success and failure. In other words, it's how you approach life in the face of adversity that builds resilience.

Where to get support

- Psychology Today – www.psychologytoday.com/us/blog/microaggressions-in-everyday-life/201010/racial-microaggressions-in-everyday-life.

- Good Therapy – www.goodtherapy.org/blog/micro aggressions-everyday-racism-in-the-21st-century-0210154.

Chapter 5

PERSONAL GROWTH

⊙ *Strong personal growth:* You have a feeling of continued development, see yourself as growing and expanding, are open to new experiences, have the sense of realising your potential, see improvement in yourself and behaviour over time and are changing in ways that reflect more self-knowledge and effectiveness.

⊙ *Weak personal growth:* You have a sense of personal stagnation, lack the sense of improvement or expansion over time, feel bored and uninterested with life and unable to develop new attitudes or behaviours.

Understanding personal growth

On reading the actor Ossie Young's eulogy to Malcolm X (X Malcolm and Haley 1965), we can take the opportunity to begin to connect and understand a little of his particular journey through life. His story reveals just how much he lived and breathed his encounters with race.

> Many will ask what Harlem finds to honour in this stormy controversial and bold young captain and will smile... Did you ever talk to him...did you ever touch him, or have him smile at you? Did you ever really listen to him? And if you knew him you would be knowing we must honour him...in honouring him we honour the best in ourselves. (X Malcolm and Haley 1965, p.76)

In Gary Younge's foreword in *The Autobiography of Malcolm X*, he describes the book as not so much the tale of a life, as the account of the personal, political and spiritual journey of a man seizing the moment and reinventing himself fashioned with deliberation. We cannot fail to be impressed with the energy and determination to live his every day immersed in a race-based narrative that stretched through every area of his life: 'Not so much a political strategy but a state of mind' (X Malcolm and Haley 1965, p.78).

What is significant for us in Malcolm X's personal account is how unique and individual he was and how much he seemed to trust his next steps into new directions without doubt or hesitation, overcoming obstacles as he strode through his life, challenging privilege and inequality. Being immersed in such activism for a whole lifetime was a particular choice for this particular man, at a particular point in history. We are navigating at a different time and in a different space. This chapter is about making steady progress towards change, and in a way living up to the best in ourselves by being open to new perspectives and new experiences. The reason I mention Malcolm X is because it serves us well to acknowledge the struggle for justice and equality; our history is a fundamental source of inspiration for our own personal growth.

Growing and expanding, however, will involve trusting your intuition – your gut feeling – in the face of those who think they know better than you about you. Being authentic and true to yourself is where you start to make progress with personal growth and this is bound to involve making mistakes. Person growth is, well, personal!

In fulfilling his calling, Malcolm X completed his mission, created a new and bigger world to live in, and provided us with a new map by which to navigate BAME lives. Not many of us have lives that will ever be remotely comparable and we don't need to aspire to resemble his journey because we have our own to contend with.

In the same way, approaching your personal growth with passion amid the spaces and places you occupy in your everyday lives is of equal importance and of equal substance. We all have ideas and aspirations that are based on our individual thinking and world views; there is no single blueprint for what makes a successful, happy, balanced individual. For one person, personal growth might be having a family and ensuring the wellbeing of loved ones to the best of their ability; for another, it may be getting a decent enough job, surviving periods of unemployment; or it could be a juggling act of many different parts of life competing for our attention.

It is easy to fall back onto the populist view that growth is what can be observed and measured as a form of advancement. Personal growth, although not divorced from material and intellectual improvement, is not reliant on this. It is much more nuanced and includes our emotional and (if relevant for you) spiritual selves. As Maya Angelou (2014, p.70) wrote, 'Since a price will be exacted from us for everything we do or leave undone, we should pluck up the courage to win back our finer and kinder healthier selves.'

Life is not a level playing field either. As a BAME person you may have to travel much further and over far rockier terrain to 'arrive' at a place in your life where you feel fulfilled and have time and space to nurture your finer, healthier self.

When considering the relationship between wellbeing and personal growth, it is helpful to ask yourself the following questions:

REFLECTION POINTS

◐ How am I growing?

◐ Where am I feeling stuck?

◐ What is holding me back?

◐ What are my achievements?

◐ Where have I exceeded my own expectation of myself?

◐ Do I have direction?

○ Am I hoping that my life will improve in some magical way or by fate?

○ Do I rely on others to direct me?

○ Where am I being blocked?

○ What is in my control?

○ What is not in my control?

These sorts of questions help to raise our self-awareness, a vital ingredient for growing well and becoming healthy.

This is not to say that you cannot be successful in life without being self-aware; however, personal growth is more than the sum of its parts. It is not only about what is projected and enacted externally, it is what you are experiencing, your emotions, deep-seated feelings of self-worth and the process of releasing your potential and giving life to it.

This is not to be confused with progression in life – it is not about you owning a car, a house and having 2.4 children; it is about being aligned to your core values and committed in yourself to creating a life that is reflective of your authentic self. If it feels like tapping into your potential is intangible and resides firmly in the future, or you have yet to formulate a particular direction or plan, there is always the opportunity to find alternative ways to express that part of yourself, to re-direct your path or to work towards a longer goal by building stepping stones, as illustrated by the case of Imran below.

Making space for continuous development

CASE STUDY

Imran is 26 years old. He has a cleaning job and looks after three or four buildings. His job mainly consists of cleaning the toilets. Imran is a practising Muslim. He openly discusses his religious views and while he 'jokes' with his secular white colleagues to make himself more acceptable in his world of work, he doesn't act this out in a way that harms his sense of self. Some of the jokes his colleagues make towards him are verging on the unacceptable – they are microaggressions he chooses to ignore in the search for his own wellbeing. He pursues his life with vigour, vitality, humour and connectedness. His daily life is full of human stories which he goes home to tell his family. He is well liked, and his ambition is to become the cleaning supervisor.

In the above case study, Imran is acting with confidence in his daily life. He has a clear idea of what he wants and how to go about achieving it. He is improving and expanding his life against many odds, such as a background of a lower economic position, limited access to a good education and therefore career opportunities and the daily weathering of microaggressions that is sometime the lived experience of BAME people in their workplace environments. Throughout his life he has held on to a sense of himself. He has a plan and is staying on course, stretching himself as much as he is able.

Whatever your current circumstances, you will always have choices about how you respond to inevitable challenges. Some choices move you in the direction you want to go, while others take you further from your destination. When you explore your options and choose one that moves things along in the direction you want to go, you start a ball rolling. This is a phased approach to change and one that will help you to focus on taking small steps towards change. It includes:

- learning to take each day as it comes

- focusing your energy where it really matters and will have an impact

- developing affirmations that keep your personal growth on track

- rewarding yourself along the way with small treats.

Imran is taking charge of his life, appearing unstoppable in his journey. He is living powerfully within the context of his circumstances and in his day-to-day activities. He is also living his life with passion, and is known for bringing exceptional vitality to his everyday activities, including making life fun for other people. He doesn't let his job description get him down or others put him down for the job he does – he commands others' respect because he so clearly respects himself. I do not advocate 'putting up and shutting up' about daily encounters with modern everyday racism and I would not be able to work in an environment where I was having to deal with so much, but I do understand that some people simply don't have the choice to move or change jobs or the support to make a complaint, because the systems in which they exist have no complaints procedures.

REFLECTION POINTS

- What would you like to change and develop in your life (choose something small)?

- Make a list of race-based injustices, inequalities and bad behaviour you have encountered?

- What would you like to do about these?

- How will what you do impact on your working life?

- How will what you do impact on your wellbeing?

- What lessons have you learned that will keep you on track with your personal growth if you make changes?

You may not be able to think of anything at this point but you could go back to these questions and reflect more at a later date. You have in a sense begun the journey by reading this book and seeking out ways to cope and manage a historical context that is not of your making. There are real barriers you may have to face, and deeply hurtful experiences of exclusion and of modern everyday racism that wound you.

Realising your potential and living above and beyond BAME categorisations

Racism makes realising your potential a demanding process. Being clear and consistent about your approach will help because, if you don't know what you want or who you want to be, or even how you are reacting and coping, then how can you grow and change? It may sound false but we all need a plan of some kind, otherwise we are going to get hopelessly lost and find ourselves without a direction of travel.

Once you have discovered a chosen destination, you will naturally find more opportunities for growth and change, and refuse to allow others or yourself to divert or sabotage your efforts. Racism in all its forms has an impact on our lives, but if you can make a decision to achieve your goals, however small, then you are more likely to succeed. If you have a map, you are simply less likely to get hopelessly lost and tangled up in other people's expectations and pressures.

REFLECTION POINTS

○ Spend some time focusing on what you want over the next month – what do you want for yourself, your family, your friends and your social environment?

○ Can you move your direction of travel positively towards something you want rather than away from something you don't want? We cannot remove racism, but we can celebrate our uniqueness, reject oppressive practices and fight for the rights of others and ourselves.

○ Consider how you would look after your wellbeing alongside the struggle for social justice?

○ The big question is: How can you grow and achieve your potential against the odds and within the structures of social injustice and racism?

Facing and welcoming new challenges

Any challenge, and particularly those faced within any race-based encounter, will make you feel under threat, anxious and unsure of yourself. The way somebody treats you may be against the law. We will be discussing race hate crime and race hate incidents later on in this chapter.

History is littered with amazing people such as Angela Davis, Audre Lorde, Toni Morrison, Steve Biko and Nelson Mandela, to name but a few. There are also the current writers and thinkers Afua Hirsh, Gary Younge, Dinesh Bhugra, Yomi Adegoke, Elizabeth Uviebiné, Reni-Eddo Lodge, all of whom have faced and welcomed their own unique challenges. But you have to face your own challenges, and your challenges are not theirs.

You may choose to focus on your health and wellbeing, letting go of any activism and deciding that 'keeping your own counsel' serves you better. Alternatively, taking the middle ground might feel safer for you, so seeking support or supporting others is also an option. Other people, like those I have listed, may choose to immerse themselves in the challenge – that is their choice and their journey, and you have the right to choose your own direction and your own response to racism. This may vary over time and in different contexts.

With this in mind, I recommend looking out for what's ahead of you. If you are caught off guard and aren't prepared for an odd comment thrown carelessly your way, how will you build a repertoire of responses? If you take regular stock of these encounters, you can build a strategy that feels right and fits with your own beliefs, values and type of personality. Even if it's only a stock response such as 'I'm sorry, I didn't quite catch that. Could you repeat it again?', it will make your microaggressor think twice before repeating their unconscious bias. But if you are not prepared and are unable to stand your ground, you could be the one left feeling disturbed, and you are not a dumping ground for the perpetrators of racism.

If you are essentially a quiet person who doesn't like being caught up in conflict, then it is counterproductive to try and become overly assertive. A process of distancing yourself from 'troublemakers' might provide a better route. Arming yourself with facts, figures and knowledge will also aid any unwanted debates, as will developing a questioning response that asks people to come up with facts and figures about the matter.

Surround yourself with supportive people and ensure there are people in your world who you can talk to freely about the impact of race-based issues on your life. You may be surprised to find that some of the people you turn to are white. Don't waste your energy with people who are not helpful and people who are seeking to undermine your experiences. Finding people to trust enough to tell your story will support your personal growth and your wellbeing.

Re-storying is a concept arising out of restorative approaches[1] and means that the process of telling and retelling your story is both necessary and healing. This approach also talks much of human needs. Focus and concentrate on yourself and your needs when facing challenges. In her book *Nonviolent Communication Companion Work Book* (2003), Leu identifies 'the universal needs that are common to all human beings' (p.179) She goes on to suggest that when are needs are left unmet, we may end up feeling: annoyed, distressed, helpless, lonely and disappointed. (p.177) But when are needs are met, we are more likely to feel comfortable, eager, hopeful, optimistic and appreciative (p.175).

A life filled with acceptance, appreciation, community, safety and consideration is one in which life's challenges will be more easily faced. It's advisable not to go it alone, not because you can't but because there is much to be gained from reaching out to others and staying connected to the people in your world.

The limits and opportunities that face us in today's world

Choosing plans and holding on to our dreams are basic needs. Some people have great clarity about where their opportunities

---

1   'A way to work through, resolve and transform conflicts in general' (Zehr 2002, p.4).

lie and what direction they would like to take. Others find their dreams and opportunities get lived out in their everyday existences – they don't need to dream big but are content with what they have. There are many ways of living a BAME life within the UK today. The trick is finding your own way, one that is unique to you and not born out of pressure from others.

Standing up for yourself/ overcoming bystander apathy

So far, we have talked much about microaggressions and forms of modern racism that are covert and almost invisible – but when BAME people get together they know exactly how to identify them and they don't need a book to define a microaggression. BAME people are calling out and naming microaggressions. People asking to touch your skin, or your hair is extremely common and not always done insensitively or committed in any wrong sense, but sometimes these forms of overstepping personal boundaries are painful and relentless. Many times, I have wanted to say, 'My hair is different – just get used to it. I have to put up with your hair being different every day too!'

Being assertive or distancing yourself in the face of constant comments about your appearance – one type of microaggression – is one thing, but being the victim of a race hate crime is another. As someone who has reported race hate crimes three times to the police and has had the experience of both verbal and physical assault, I have a considerable amount of personal knowledge about the process of reporting and what it entails.

Reporting race-based hate crime and empowerment

How do we thrive in our environments because 'Racism is intensely painful and has an adverse impact on the social, economic, psychological, physical and mental well-being of those who experience it. Very few people would argue otherwise' (Sewell 2009, p.182).

So how do we overcome the obstacles life throws in our direction? How do we grow out of our comfort zones and venture towards creating the life we would wish for? What are the limits and opportunities our current social and cultural context place on us? What are we facing in terms of everyday experiences of racism, where discrimination is handed out consciously and unconsciously, covertly and overtly, when as Kandola so poignantly describes, 'The simple act of being oneself can be interpreted as a wilful act of challenge' (2009, p.88)?

The current political climate is changing apace, and post-Brexit the landscape feels less safe for everyone. As a result, it is even more important to find people who have faced similar experiences to you and who will support you in finding ways out of habitually reacting to racism in old familiar patterns. It's not that these patterns of reacting are mistaken, but you may need to develop new strategies, new ways of ensuring your own growth, realising your potential and expanding your world. Complaining and always being up against the system is not enough to live a fruitful life. Kandola sums up the conundrum:

> People are reluctant to complain about being excluded because they do not want to be labelled as troublemakers…we all have a strong impulse not to rock the boat…even when we have the sense the boat is heading for the rocks. (Kandola 2009, p.100)

This chapter is not about 'exposing racism' – we know it exists and is deep seated and woven into the fabric of our society and culture – but is written in the hope we can find ways of creatively existing within this culture, finding our own way through the white spaces that seek to narrowly define and restrict our options.

Emerging from everyday experiences of racism without scars is a tall order. We have no control over whether we become victims of exclusionary practices, and life goes on whatever the most up-to-date management strategies or legislation set out to deliver.

Becoming aware of choice and change involves making individual decisions, even though the status quo remains solid. We cannot afford to live our lives waiting for the arrival of an inclusive culture, waiting for an understanding that social justice is not an add-on but an essential ingredient for all healthy societies.

Gael Lindenfield and Malcolm Vandenburg (2000, p.36) describe a process of wanting change, thinking about change acting on change, feeling the change and lastly being the change.

To illustrate how this process works in action, here is an example:

CASE STUDY

Akash is 35 years old and works for a major company. He is the only Muslim British Bangladeshi within his department. He feels very isolated and out of touch with his family and his culture. He feels encouraged to talk about his experiences with his colleagues but also feels that every conversation is linked to his being a Muslim, and his religious views are constantly being challenged and questioned under the cover of banter. He has also held himself back out of fear that assertiveness coming from a British Bangladeshi will be viewed negatively and he will be measured by unfair standards. He has decided he wants to change and to be more assertive in relation to the role he is playing in the workplace. He has researched assertiveness on the internet and ordered a book he feels might really help him begin to cope with what is being projected onto him. He has found some assertiveness strategies that involve not being a passive victim of invasive questioning but rather learning how to become 'questioning', that is, to question back in equal measure and with equal degrees of over-familiarity. He has kept a notebook of responses he has made and practises them as much as he can. He is now being more effective in his work and is enjoying everything about his work because he feels more in control of his responses. Not only has he become more approachable, but he is also more approaching. Learning to ask for what he needs and responding openly has made a direct impact on his personal growth.

Akash has made a decision to change and we can see clearly how he has proceeded through the five stages:

1. *Want it* – He wants to make an effective difference to his own life and the way in which he responds.

2. *Think it* – He is practising being assertive.

3. *Act it* – He is now acting differently with his colleagues.

4. *Feel it* –He is feeling more in control and more contented at work.

5. *Be it* – He is now being more productive and is being assertive.

As Kieran Yates, in the stunningly moving book, *The Good Immigrant*, points out, we 'have been too busy being good immigrants, not making a fuss, and quieting down when people feel uncomfortable' (Shukla 2016, p.118).

Learning to express yourself better and becoming clearer about what you are seeing, hearing and sensing help you regain a sense of belonging. Being anchored into the conversation is probably better than allowing yourself to drift in silence waiting for a miracle.

Empowering yourself

Sometimes you may need to change your environment to distance yourself from absorbing too much of the bias unconsciously handed out. Exploring new ways of thinking, doing and being will provide a way of feeling less stuck with something you as an individual cannot change.

If we believe that each new phase of life presents both losses and opportunities, we will find creative ways to better transform our lives. The reflection points will help you clarify your thoughts, bringing them into consciousness. Writing things down will also help this process.

REFLECTION POINTS

○ What is it like being a BAME person in the UK?

○ What are your thoughts and feelings about this?

○ What impact do these thoughts, feelings and behaviours have on your wellbeing?

○ What would you like to change or to shift a lot or a little?

○ What feels possible and not possible?

○ How have you grown and changed over time in relation to your experiences?

○ What would it feel like to change it more?

Conscious change is energised by maintaining a clear picture of where you are now and of what you want in the future and the choices that are available to you. Each turning point in your life is a milestone, a time of loss and a time of new beginnings.

The comfort zone

Our relationship with stress can reveal much about how we perceive the world. High levels of stress, especially over a sustained period of time, can result in a sort of numbing, known in psychology as dissociation, a blanking out of the senses to cope with what is going on. In the field of trauma, it is called 'freezing' and can be a terrifying experience. Richard Dienstbier's (1989) theory of mental toughness suggests that experiencing some manageable stressors, with recovery in between, can make us mentally tough and less reactive to future stress. This may partly be because these experiences enable us to view stressors as more manageable and we become more skillful at dealing with them.

At the other end of the spectrum, no stress at all can result in a 'rusting' of our brain and neglect of our latent potential. Can you recall a time when you felt utterly bored and trapped? Perhaps it was at school or in a job you hated? For me, it was a bit like holding my breath under water and surfacing only when I had got myself out of that dead-end, uninspiring environment.

A way of looking at this is through the comfort zone exercise, which is a simple way of understanding how you approach new learning, novel experiences and what scares you!

We are probably all familiar with the phrase 'in my comfort zone'. Such a lovely cosy phrase, it is the equivalent of a warm, fluffy, emotional blanket wrapped around us as protection from the winds of change! Mine is my bedroom, my candlelit sanctuary where I read, watch the clouds pass over the moon at night and listen to the tawny owl in the woods beside my house.

Where is your comfort zone? Imagine you are there right now – what can you smell, sense, feel? The problem is, we can't live in our comfort zone all the time. It's a great place to recharge and to feel a sense of orderliness in the world but we need more variety in our lives to make our lives worth living and to enhance our personal growth.

THE COMFORT ZONE EXERCISE

Get a piece of paper – the larger the better – and draw a circle in the middle, not too big. Inside the circle, write the things you do that you are completely and utterly comfortable with. It could be things like walking the dog, going to the cinema, going to choir practice. This is your Comfort Zone.

Now draw a circle around this first circle, leaving a gap, and write in things you can do but you have to give yourself a bit of a push to do them – activities or experiences that are a little bit challenging, but not so much that you are put off. This might include learning a new language, hosting a dinner party for friends, putting a flat-pack set of drawers together. This is your Growth Zone.

Draw a third circle around the second circle and write in things you would like to do but you lack courage with. This may be starting a business, writing a book, travelling to Thailand on your own. This is your Fear Zone.

Draw a fourth circle around the third and include activities, experiences or goals that completely terrify you but you would like to do one day. This may be things like deep-sea diving, applying for a specialist department post as a junior member of staff, settling down! This is your Panic Zone.

You can draw additional circles if you like, and give them a zone name.

Make sure that what you include is a reflection of your personal situation, activities, hopes, dreams and fears, not what you think other people want or expect from you.

When you have completed your zones, spend some time considering and writing down where your fear resides and where you have created comfortable non-threatening routines/habits in your daily life.

Remember, this exercise is for you and about you; it's not what you think other people would expect or request you to do.

- Is there anything in your comfort zone that might have started off in one of the outer zones?

- Are you able to expand your comfort zone to include things in your growth zone? What would you need to do this? What small steps could you take?

- Are you able to take something from your fear zone and look at it in a different way? What is scaring you? Who could you get help from to build confidence in this area? Are you imagining the worst? Are you being put off by the thought of failure?

The concept of being out of our comfort zone doesn't have to scare us. It can be incredibly exciting and fulfilling to feel the fear and do it anyway, and you can expand your zones over a period of time in a way that is manageable for you. In fact, the lines in between the zones are called the 'growing edge' and this is where our most significant growth happens, on the verge of excitement and fear. If we can harness the excitement rather than be consumed by fear or self-criticism, we are more likely to succeed and make progress, growing in confidence at the same time. This is not about walking in a straight line – you may have to pick yourself up and dust yourself off many times in the process.

If you have a fear of public speaking, for example, you could start off by speaking to a small group to try your material out, or record a video or produce a leaflet. Incrementally, you may want to build up to a public-speaking engagement by researching the best way to project your voice and how to hold yourself with confidence. You may decide to ask someone you think is a great public speaker to work with you. You may record your voice and listen back to it, noticing not only what you need to improve on but how well you come across in places.

Growth does not have to happen in one big leap – you can make those scary goals into more workable zones by breaking them down into bite-sized chunks. If you find yourself being put off by perfectionism or procrastination, challenge yourself to start anyway and stay with it even through self-judgement and not knowing – it is not in the successes that we learn the most about ourselves, it is through our failures and how we pick ourselves up.

Experiences of racism put us in touch with our powerlessness and our vulnerability – even more so when we are trying move from our comfort zones.

In his book, *Cross Cultural Psychiatry*, Dinesh Bhugra writes that 'racist persecutions or individual racist assaults form part of the social reality for black and ethnic minority groups' and he goes on to say that 'such acts without doubt create distress for the targets of the assault' (Bhugra and Bhui 2001, p.96). But we can cushion the blow of such transitions by building our resources when things are going well. Such measures might include managing our finances/resources, planning future events with friends and family, cooking and looking after our physical selves, changing our diet, taking up some form of exercise and developing new interests, some challenging and some less challenging. We always have some control over a difficult event and this might mean being brave enough to ask for help.

We may also find that familiar patterns and ways of behaving are no longer working for us. For example, you may be continuously told that you are 'worthless' in this society, but feel that overnight change is often too complex and demanding. Widening your horizons by turning away from being and feeling only defined by the colour of your skin or your cultural background is no easy feat. You may need time to discover how you want to live, what needs you have and how to meet them, and how you want to be in the world. We have no control over how and why others project their views on to us, whether that be overtly or covertly, but we can and we must form a clear picture of where we want to be.

Negotiating change will inevitably bring with it an element of anxiety; but the more we practise changing, the stronger we will become and the more we will look forward to a different future, however small that change might be.

The link between reporting race hate crime and empowerment

In this section I will reveal some of my own experiences of race hate crime. In recent years, I have changed the way in which I respond to being a target of racial abuse, because I have learned to begin to trust the process of reporting hate crime.

Being the target of racial abuse can provoke a range of responses. We are not all the same and we will not all respond in the same way. Being a target of hate crime is distressing and traumatic, and a well-documented outcome of victims of hate crime is that they restrict their everyday lives, staying safe to feel safe; for example, not going out at night, or not going to certain places and changing the way they dress to attempt to fit in and be less visible. This is a perfectly normal response, but restricting your life for prolonged periods of time is most likely an unhealthy response and it would be best to seek the support of your GP if you feel like this.

If you have experiences of racism in your childhood – be they minor aggressions or major injuries – your wellbeing and sense of self-worth are bound to have been affected.

Continuous verbal and physical assault experienced in some BAME communities shape some of our lives, promoting messages that we do not belong and that many people in the UK would prefer us to 'go home'; these are mixed with the messages of deportation. And all this amid the paradoxes of revering the English football team and stars like Michael Jackson, Beyoncé and Stormzy. That countless white people who swarm to their concerts casually throw out racist remarks to passers-by is not an irony missed by BAME people.

We walk endlessly in and out of crowds of white spaces daily. I have a vague fear and am watchful as soon as I leave my front door, because in certain parts of the country safety and normality do not exist and I have been caught off-guard too many times.

A personal account

I was 9 years old and had caught the bus home and was now walking through the bus station at 4.00 in the afternoon. A man who appeared to be in his thirties stuck his leg out between my feet and tackled me to the ground. I fell sprawled on the concrete, so shocked that for a few moments I could not get up and was hoping from the depths of my heart that someone would come to my aid. But deep in my heart I already knew that nobody would. I already had an inborn unhealthy resilience to such attacks and rose to my feet, my forehead cut and bleeding into my eye, both knees bleeding onto white socks, hand raw as I had reached out to save myself. I decided not to cry and not to feel as I had many times before. And yet another day's experience of being 'thrown against a sharp white background' (Rankine 2014, p.53) and weathered by its endlessness. As my mind began to shut down, I also became aware that my response was flattening the life out of me and limiting my spirit.

'Another friend tells you you have to learn not to absorb the world. She says sometimes she can hear her own voice saying silently to whomever – you are saying this thing and I am not going to accept it.' (Rankine 2014, p.55)

There are no happy endings to encounters with racism such as the one I describe above and there are scars that have never healed and doubtless never will. Since then, I have experienced countless verbal and physical assaults on a micro and macro level. It was only when I became aware that statistics were being held by various government institutions on the reporting of race hate crime that I plucked up the courage to start to report my own. My first attempts were useless and the police at the end of the phone were unable to respond – they clearly had no training and lacked awareness. And now I have reported a crime and had the perpetrator arrested, I have received support from the police, been interviewed by the police and have come away from that experience for the first time in my life with a sense of empowerment.

What is a hate crime?

Understanding the Difference: The Initial Police Response to Hate Crime is a recent report from Her Majesty's Inspectorate of Constabulary and Fire and Rescue Services (2018), providing information and comments on the police response to hate crime in the UK. The report shows that racial hate crime represents the largest motivating factor for recorded hate crime, accounting for 70 per cent of all motivating factors in 2016/2017. The police specifically monitor if a person is targeted because of a disability, race, ethnicity, religion or belief, sexual orientation, transgender identity or alternative subcultures. In addition to this, anyone can be a victim of hate crime – you don't need to be a member of a minority group.

The report also states that there is strong evidence to suggest that hate crime is significantly under-reported across all categories. It usefully defines a hate crime and a hate incident as follows:

Hate crime: A criminal offence which is perceived by the victim, or any other person, to be motivated by hostility or prejudice towards someone based on personal characteristics. (p.97)

Hate incident: An incident, that does not amount to a criminal offence, which is perceived by the victim, or any other person, to be motivated by hostility or prejudice towards someone based on a personal characteristic. (p.98)

Hate incidents can be recorded where there is no evidence available but there is a perception that an incident has taken place.

Overt and abusive forms of racism that could be defined as either an incident or a hate crime might include:

- Verbal abuse

- Verbal bullying

- Ridiculing and stereotyping

- Receiving racist hate messages through social media (cyberbullying), including messages, spreading rumours, pictures and unkind comments related to race – they can be sent round to other groups or within groups of colleagues or friends

- Damage to property

- Physical violence and threats of violence.

Increases in hate crime

Understanding the Difference (Her Majesty's Inspectorate of Constabulary and Fire and Rescue Services 2018) points to a large increase in recorded hate crimes every year since records began in 2011/12. It suggests that the increase may show a genuine rise in hate crime or may be due to a combination of three reasons:

- More people coming forward to report hate crimes that have been committed.

- Improved recording practices by the police.

The report also highlights the sharp increase in the number of racially or religiously aggravated offences following these events:

- Murder of Lee Rigby, May 2013

- Increased conflict in Israel and Gaza, July 2014

- Charlie Hebdo shooting, January 2015

- Paris attacks, 2015

- Beginning of the EU referendum campaign and again after the results in June 2016.

Reporting a race hate crime

Directly call the police as a 999 call in an emergency situation. Or call 101 in a non-emergency. Reporting a race hate crime is a brave step to take and I advise seeking support from the charities listed below and from trusted friends or colleagues. It might be tempting to 'go it alone' and for some this may be a better approach, but for most people, seeking support and advice will be a significant benefit to wellbeing.

What to expect from the police

When you make the initial call to the police, it is useful to have an understanding of what to expect. First and foremost, you should expect a high standard of service and a considered approach to your unique circumstances. The police will have a series of questions they will ask you and they will give you an incident number. Making sure you are given an incident number is very important as it will act as a reference for you to keep, and it logs the call with the police.

Expect to be asked information about the perpetrators and the incident itself – what happened and who the people were. You might also be asked if you have been a victim before. Although this may feel irrelevant, the police will be trying to find out whether or not there is a pattern and if what happened before impacted on your health and wellbeing. They will also try to determine whether or not you are still at risk of harm through a repeated targeting. Gathering this information will make it possible to categorise the risk as low, medium or high. Collecting information, assessing the risk to you and attempting to quantify the likelihood of the risk occurring again are all important aspects of the reporting process. The police may need to put safeguarding actions in place to minimise or eradicate any more risk to you or to the wider community.

You should expect regular, supportive contact with the police. During this process you may be asked how you feel, if you are frightened of further injury and if you are isolated from family and friends. They will want to know if you are depressed, anxious or suicidal. These are all perfectly normal questions and a part of a process that is there to help you to feel safe and secure. Feeling safe is a fundamental human necessity, particularly when you have been a victim of hate crime. The police service will take into account your individual circumstances – for example, it might be appropriate to offer you a translator or to help you communicate in different formats and languages.

You should also expect to receive follow-up support and to be signposted to organisations in your area that can also offer you support. Your situation should be adequately assessed as you could be targeted again. The police may have specialist hate crime staff who may visit you and offer specific support. You are entitled to an enhanced service as you will be deemed to have been the victim of a serious crime. A priority for the police will be to build a good relationship with you by listening to you and hearing and respecting all you have to say.

If you have been the victim of hate but this does not amount to a crime, it will be logged and taken seriously as an incident. This is where a great deal of confusion is caused for the victim and it is also a critical point at which the police response might vary.

Most hate crimes that get to court are where a criminal offence has been committed.

Hate-motivated victimisation often involves 'low level' and escalating acts of harassment, verbal abuse, general forms of intimidation and ongoing victimisation over protracted periods of time. This can lead to many different forms of psychological distress, which is is a perfectly normal response. It's worthwhile seeking out support as soon as you are able to. It's important to see your GP in the event of a serious incident or where you feel worn down over a long period of time.

Other support and reporting services

Online support is available through organisations such as:

- True Vision – www.report-it.org.uk

- Tell Mama – https://tellmamauk.org

- Stop Hate Uk – www.stophateuk.org

- The Community Security Trust – community security trust

- Kidscape – https://www.kidscape.org.uk/news/2016/june/united-against-all-forms-of-bullying-and-abuse

You may experience forms of anxiety or depression or begin to adapt your everyday life because you are too nervous to, for example, walk near the place you were targeted, see friends or go to work – all of which are natural responses to being targeted in this way. These new behaviours might feel safer and are justifiable for a while, but should you experience prolonged changes or thoughts and feelings that are intruding on your wellbeing, then you need to seek the support of your GP.

My decision to report race hate crimes grew out of an increase in my confidence and feelings of personal power. I have since reported race hate crimes on three occasions. I'm not going to underestimate the many feelings this provoked in me. These were mainly anxiety and concern that I would not be believed and that my experience was insignificant and irrelevant to the police – and the vague feeling that my actions were somehow inappropriate. I would like to stress that this change in me regarding reporting did not happen overnight – it was a slow build-up of confidence and knowledge. I gradually understood that even if an individual police member was not on my side, I knew enough about the law to be confident enough to go through the process.

The third time this occurred, I was with a white male friend, walking in the centre of town in the middle of the day. My friend and I felt deeply shocked by this targeted attack, so much so that we were initially confused and did not walk away as soon as it happened. However, my previous experience of this kind of thing had given me the confidence to switch out of shock mode and into action mode. I suggested to my friend we go to the police station and report it. I cannot say the process from reporting to the outcome was trouble-free and painless – making a statement to the police is emotionally gruelling and time consuming. Hearing that the perpetrator has been arrested and the circumstances of their arrest and questioning brings up a mixture of feelings, and awaiting the outcome from the Crown Prosecution Service is a very stressful and difficult time.

Certain coping skills can sustain you through the stages mentioned above:

- *Reach out to others* – Having a friend and a witness to support you can be both enabling and encouraging.

- *Relax and exercise* – Sticking to a healthy diet and continuing to exercise as you would do normally can prevent you from slipping into other less healthy coping mechanisms.

- *Be assertive* – Having a clear understanding that people no longer have the right to exert this form of power and control over you in the form of verbal threats helps enomously.

- *Believe that you can change* – I found it empowering to take action and then to get support for the actions I had taken.

- *Learn from your experience and new knowledge to support other people who may have been through similar experiences but fear reporting* – Helping others will increase your wellbeing and self-worth.

- *Redefine your priorities* – In this instance, my priorities were not necessarily about gaining a conviction but more to do with making sure I did not withdraw and diminish my self-esteem and my hard-won confidence by limiting my actions.

- *Maximise the good parts of the change and minimise the downside* – The support from my friend was vitally important and in this case the support and action from the police strongly influenced my view of their procedures. I have since supported others in reporting incidents.

- *Research organisations that might help you* – There are organisations that can help and act as an advocate if necessary.

- *Make the most of community resources* – It is helpful to find out what support there is in the community. Religious and community leaders/members could be forms of support. Make sure these organisations are not following their own agendas and are overly motivated by politics or religion (unless you have made a conscious choice about this). Strong feelings can sometimes help but can also overwhelm you to a point that you end up taking on the other person's feelings rather than your own. The idea that 'bad things should never happen' comes from a sense of privilege that I have certainly never felt; and outrage is not a feeling I have experienced when living through everyday racism (although this is often the loud call from people who have not lived through it). Strong feelings from others can interfere with your own individual processing and it is this flow of thoughts and feelings that need the comfort of our attention and the comfort from others. Outrage sometimes has a place, but it is not generally a great comforter.

- *Be able to turn to family and friends safely and without being judged* – Make considered choices and find friends who will listen to you and not necessarily overreact or underreact. To have someone listen to you and be able to mind their own reactions and feelings until you have had the chance to express yours is the best outcome. It's important to deal with your own responses and not end up managing other people's overriding expressions of emotion.

- *Know what actions will increase your wellbeing* – In my case, this was about: reporting the incident, and through the process receiving and accepting the right kind of support; feeling proud and empowered by taking action against the perpetrators; understanding that 'reporting' benefits the local community and keeps everyone safe; taking advice and listening to the police about ways of protecting myself; collecting evidence; taking photos while safe; learning what is useful when giving a description; and looking out for immediate help and making sure I was safe.

- *Know what actions will hurt your wellbeing* – Not looking after yourself both physically and emotionally can make you withdrawn and emotionally isolated. *Are there any actions you could take today that would increase your personal power?*

- *Let go of past negative perceptions of yourself* – Don't become overly focused on or influenced by what has happened. Part of the process of doing this would be to form clear images, perhaps intentions, of how you will support your wellbeing, your sense of self and your future growth. A kind of dusting yourself off and not absorbing the negativity of the event.

I am not suggesting that I did not feel frightened or have some fear about going out into public situations. For a period after the event, my immediate response was to withdraw to give myself time to regain solid ground and confidence, knowing that increased anxiety was a natural and totally necessary consequence. To be made to feel in such a public way that you do not belong within the society in which you live is still astonishing.

Since Brexit, we have seen a rise in crimes motivated by race and religious hate directed towards identifiable groups and motivated by hostility such as Islamophobia. The spike in the reporting of these crimes is undeniable and is possibly the consequence of a criminal minority feeling emboldened to act out and to openly appear justified to abuse others in covert and conscious ways.

The experience of everyday racism in my life has eroded my confidence and self-esteem many times, but through these experiences I have grown in new directions, become more resilient, taken on challenges and learned new things about myself and the world I live in.

Racism appears to be mixed up with current government legislation that on the one hand espouses equality and celebrates diversity and on the other seeks to exploit BAME communities, as demonstrated by the recent electoral process.

> The EU referendum result has perhaps emboldened racists by leading them to believe that the majority agree with their views on immigration and legitimising such public expressions of hatred. For this, the political elite must take responsibility, after stoking a divisive referendum campaign that demonised immigrants by spreading fictitious scare stories, all the while pandering to the lowest common denominator. (Versi 2016)

It is still notable how hard it is to talk about racism within any context or institution within this country. This amounts to a daily regeneration of racism in the minds of those only too willing to have their stereotypes and biases reinforced.

A meaningful life will necessarily entail acting for something larger than yourself and recognising what you add and value in your world. It is helpful to find a purpose that goes beyond merely meeting your own needs. That could even be something like joining a community garden or volunteering project – there are practical steps we can take to make meaning, and we do not have to go for the grand gestures. Maintaining strong connections to family, friends and the community, whether that be online or offline, meets many personal needs and provides plenty of space to grow. The downside of groups of people is that they have expectations and codes of behaviour that can feel restrictive when there is something you want to do but the group doesn't approve. As Robertson (2012, p.256) says, 'Resilience means remaining committed to acting in accord with personal values, at a practical level, despite everything that life throws at you.'

There is a balance to be found between meeting your own needs and contributing to others. Facing the dangers of race-based discrimination takes communities.

Where to get support

- British Association for Counselling and Psychotherapy – www.bacp.co.uk/about-therapy/what-therapy-can-help-with.

- Black History Month – www.blackhistorymonth.org.uk.

Chapter **6**

PURPOSE IN LIFE

○ *Strong purpose in life:* You have goals in life and a sense of directedness, feel there is meaning to your present and past life, hold beliefs that give life purpose and have aims and objectives for living.

○ *Weak purpose in life:* You lack a sense of meaning in life, have few goals or aims, lack a sense of direction, do not see purpose in your past life and have no outlook or beliefs that give life meaning.

Reaching above and beyond the context in which we live and learning to become more ourselves in our encounters with everyday racism to some extent involves living a worthwhile life beyond the racialised context, without ignoring its existence and its impact on our life. Alongside this, we would do well to set about discovering our aims and objectives for living. Finding purpose in life calls for us to avoid internalising other people's expectations and demands, as well as to remind ourselves that we are not the problem, although the context in which we live may give rise to the problems we experience.

Direct and indirect messages are passed down to BAME people to try to fit in, not to look too different and to appear as mainstream as possible. The pressure to conform is born from the fear that looking different and being too different will bring about a negative response and even prevent success in life. Young BAME people also face particular pressure to achieve academically and choose subjects both at school and college that are valued over others.

Over the last 20 years of my working life I have noticed discernible themes as to what gets in the way of aims and goals. The barriers seem to amount to pressure to conform, and pressure to live up to traditional family values and norms while negotiating the mainstream, as well as working harder, getting better grades and going along with a level of acceptance even when being disadvantaged.

Self-preservation and self-protection are also key themes when seeking outside help from healthcare professionals, who may have little understanding of the impact of racism, and narrow and simplistic agendas around healthcare provision.

Where our 'cultural, social and political lives may be outside the experience of most of their colleagues, to such an extent that they feel unable to share histories…for fear of being judged and labelled' (Cousins 2011, p.12). It is always worth finding the right kind of professionals to support you. Health care professionals need to be able to hear your experience of racism and they need to be able to listen without defensiveness or judgement.

Many BAME people have learned to keep their voices at bay and in the shadows.

Real dialogue seems to be disappearing within a sea of current clinical and competitive management systems. But supportive, humorous, generous and warm-hearted relationships are key elements that make up the best teams in any workplace; in any other setting and in my experience, they are also the most productive.

That said, there are many examples of good practice in all our institutions where allies, activists and genuinely committed people are working for social justice in all areas of UK life. We have forums, we have places and spaces where we can speak – even though these are still tense landscapes, there is much to be proud of and more work to be done. BAME people 'should not be expected to edit their experiences and self-expression in order to "fit in". Ultimately being unable to express oneself freely results in unhappiness, a lack of wellbeing, mental and/or physical ill health' (Cousins 2011, p.16).

The higher education sector has Eurocentric views woven into the fabric of its curriculums. If we are going to mirror young people's world views we need to move away from such rigid perspectives. History, literature, art and science did not just take place in the western world; there are other perspectives too numerous to mention and there are other witnesses to the historical account we have written in the name of others.

There is a whole heap of meaning in your past and present life and your personal history, and to gain a clearer picture of that meaning it would be worth reflecting on where you are headed and where you came from. Knowing where you are headed and your direction of travel will provide you with a source of strength, and if we think about it and act on it, like any other journey it will slowly become an automatic way of thinking. Take, for example, getting up and going to work – we don't have to think about it because we do it every day. So if your aim was to get more involved in local community activities and you decided how much time to give the new venture, what day you would give up to do it and so on, after you had been involved for six months the activity would become second nature, and to a certain extent become embedded in your life's routine.

REFLECTION POINTS

- How would you like your life to be?

- Where in your life do you feel connected, inspired, motivated?

- Have you neglected any passions and pastimes that you previously enjoyed and that connected you to yourself?

- What are the everyday activities you might do – cooking, meeting up with friends, cleaning, managing your home – that you may not value but are small acts of self-care that accumulate to make a significant impact on your wellbeing?

- Can you compose a vision of where you would like to be in five years' time?

I don't mean these to come across as a list of socially aspirational questions. Some of our lives are restricted by lack a of resources, financial stability, accommodation needs and so on. These are basic needs that must be taken care of. Neglected pastimes and interests may not be feasible for you at this point. We live in a social hierarchy where homelessness and poverty are on the increase and finding meaning under these circumstances may well be solely about finding that meaning in survival.

BAME people face a bias that is essentially constructed by the dominant culture. We have no control over its current expression but we do have some control over how we make meaning out of our everyday lives. It is almost impossible to overcome how other people view you, or indeed how you view yourself. Nevertheless, we need not feel totally overwhelmed and attached to the inevitable emotional struggles that come with the territory. If society is busy creating and making meaning for us through stereotypes, through forms of unconscious bias, and through all forms of media, we can at the very least try to find meaning within our own lives. It is simply not enough to have a life continually determined from the outside as an outsider. As Kandola (2009) suggests, 'Diversity is not a problem: it's a fact and far from being a measure of complexity or difficulty, diversity is a factor of strength' (p.219).

Very few of us come into this world having an innate calling to something profound. There are people who find a path that suits them and they hone this skill or passion over many years until it looks essentially effortless. You are a person embedded within a network of relationships, influenced by tendencies related to past, present and future events within an ever-changing racially charged landscape. The process of finding a way through this terrain can be life-enhancing and engender the ability to protect, to adjust, to challenge and to develop a new sense of purpose.

Purpose can sound like a big responsibility. To be purposeful is to be attentive, hardworking and gifted, to have clarity and stamina – all fine attributes, and they certainly have a place in a version of purpose; but in relation to wellbeing, having purpose is better described as seeking and finding meaning in life.

Purposeful pause

In his book, *Don't Sweat the Small Stuff...and It's All Small Stuff*, Richard Carlson (2008) invites you to imagine that when you wake in the morning, before the day begins and you get swept upstream on a current of busyness and mental chatter, you pause and take a few seconds to ask yourself this question: What's really important?

Reminding yourself of what is important to you helps to keep your priorities straight. In spite of your responsibilities, you still have a choice as to where you put your time and energy in the present moment and perhaps you will also find that some of your choices are in conflict with your life goals.

To build your resilience, plan action in accordance with your most cherished values and priorities (Robertson 2012).

Connecting with your purpose

The meaning you give to your life permeates every part of your existence. Embracing and crafting meaning, even if we have to mine very deep for it, can help us to connect with our purpose. To create meaning is to have a love for something or someone that gives us a reason to live.

Living a meaningful life is one in which we:

- have a reason to get up in the morning

- feel alive within and have passion for something

- are inspired by something (even if occasionally)

- experience joy, hope and a sense of belonging

- feel excited about future possibilities

- don't blame our past actions or behaviours but see them as growth

- know that we can contribute to the world in some way

- make the most of our talents and skills

- feel gratitude

- have something to look forward to

- have an opportunity to express some form of creativity

- are able to support ourselves emotionally through hard times

- have fun.

In this respect, we do not find purpose in what we do but in who we are. Being authentic to yourself and being *you* is living purposefully. The way in which you get there is to some extent incidental, whether it be through your work, community or some type of pursuit – honouring *yourself* is allowing personal meaning and a sense of purpose to thrive.

The difficulty arises when we have not sufficiently connected with our individual sense of purpose or we have lost our way. Feeling disconnected from our inner self and finding solace through distraction, escapism and ways to numb our emotional self can arise, as can depression and lethargy.

According to the Japanese, everyone has an *ikigai* – a reason for being. In the handbook *Ikigai: The Japanese Secret to a Long and Happy Life* (2017) Héctor Garcia and Francesc Miralles explain that some people have found their *ikigai* while others are still looking, though they carry it within them. Our *ikigai* is hidden within us and finding it requires a patient search.

One way to start the process of uncovering your *ikigai* is to draw four circles with overlaps:

Circle 1: What you love.

Circle 2: What the world needs.

Circle 3: What you can get paid for.

Circle 4: What you are good at.

Figure 6.1: Finding your ikigai
Based on a diagram by Mark Winn

The overlaps represent your passion, mission, vocation and profession.

Questions to ask yourself while undertaking this exercise are:

1. *What drives me?* – What do I love to do, what makes me feel alive, motivated, moved? Is there something that touches me so deeply and I need to play a part as an agent for change or a healer?

2. *What energises me?* – What gives me energy rather than depleting me of energy?

3. *What am I willing to sacrifice?* – Am I willing to forgo anything to achieve this?

4. *Who do I want to help?* – Is there a specific group, type of person or movement I want to be involved with that I feel drawn to?

5. *How can I get there?* – What do I need to do to acquire the skills or take steps to get where I want to be?

Finding purpose, either big or small, is a lifelong journey and you will change along the way; you will re-evaluate and at times feel a bit lost and overwhelmed. This is normal, as you are a work in progress, not the finished article. However, we need to be aware that normal thoughts and feelings can tip over into experiencing stress or low mood. These are are a part of the ups and downs of life, but if they develop into depression and anxiety, this could lead on to experiencing mental health problems. It can be really challenging to be on the receiving end of microaggressions, prejudice, hate incidents or crimes (Carlson 2008; Garcia and Miralles 2017).

The experience of facing racism on a personal and structural level is without doubt a cause of distress in the lives of BAME people. How we deal with that distress depends on many factors, and whether that distress edges towards depression, anxiety or forms of psychosis depends on varied and multiple factors. Until now there has been little research in this area.

I have witnessed levels of anxiety and depression in the lives of BAME people who have been the targets of both overt and covert forms of racism. Most commonly this has been BAME people adapting and changing behaviours in order to increase their feelings of safety and levels of trust towards society. However, this has also been people developing symptoms of agoraphobia and post-traumatic stress disorder having experienced the intense emotions that result from trauma.

How we experience racism

Feeling safe is a basic human need. We cannot function if we do not feel safe, and we are bound to experience forms of anxiety if we don't live or work in environments where safety from all forms of threat is available. It seems clear that being a constant object of racism makes life more stressful, both on an unconscious and conscious level. Throughout this book I have attempted to direct you towards healthier ways of managing your wellbeing within a sometimes hostile environment. Developing healthy protective strategies as a consequence of being raised in racist environments is normal. Managing the conflicting demands of fitting in with different cultures and with the people we spend most of our time with is a balancing and challenging act. We can reduce the impact racism has on our wellbeing to some extent but this very much depends on the severity of our experience, and on social and economic factors.

BAME people may never experience any forms of racism; however, they may experience a one-off incident, regular incidents, persistent and harmful incidents, acute and traumatic incidents (Lago and Barbara 2003, p.23).

Any of these experiences may cause you to have a reaction that may leave you unable to cope with the problem on your own and you may experience levels of anxiety or depression that escalate extremely quickly. In these circumstances, you need to get help by going to your GP as soon as you can, and in the case of serious physical or emotional assault go to the emergency department at a hospital. Exposure to any kind of trauma creates a stress response that can lead us to experience intense emotions that are all the more frightening because of their unfamiliarity.

The experience of trauma or prolonged experiences of abuse can have a serious impact on your mental health and on your ability to cope. Being in a state of permanent anxiety can cause significant stress and eventual breakdown, as can low mood, loss of interest in life and withdrawing from friends and family.

In the immediate aftermath of a serious incident, seek help as soon as you can.

Seeking help from people you trust to listen to you without judgement and without questioning is a fundamental starting point. People who are able to remain calm, let go of their own agendas and be there for you whatever you decide to do are definitely the kind of people you need around you.

Sometimes healthcare providers – nurses, GPs, counsellors and wellbeing practitioners – fail to connect with your experience and may:

- Be unable to make sense of your distress because they do not understand the experience of racism and have no understanding of the power dynamics of racism.

- Be unprepared to listen and build an understanding of your lived experience of racism, and instead question your reality. The types of questions you may be asked essentially add up to you having to prove the incident was racist.

- Replicate discriminatory practices by denying your experience.

- Minimise your experience through paying less attention to matters of importance to the patient (Bhui 2002, p.212).

- Overreact to your experience in such a way that their response becomes the focus of the conversation.

As Bhui (2002, p.212) writes: '[If] personal pain such as racism is denied by societies' sanctioned help-givers, a final breach in trust will arise. Individuals at the height of personal distress experience being categorised inaccurately – repeating a trauma of non-recognition'.

The above examples of bad practice within healthcare environments are not here to stop you from seeking the support you deserve and need, but acknowledging and preparing for the impact of the kind of microaggressions you may face when seeking help is an important part of the process of healing and processing your experiences. Again, I suggest that you take a trusted friend with you; whether they are white or BAME, it doesn't matter. The only consideration if you become ill is that the person or people who you chose to help you do not deny or minimise your experience.

Aside from having an awareness that healthcare professionals may get it wrong – and in some cases very wrong – when you feel you are becoming ill or developing more serious aspects of depression, anxiety or post-traumatic stress disorder, you need to seek help. Your priority under these circumstances is to get treatment, not to challenge the status quo. What you need to do is:

- seek the support of a friend, family or community

- attend an emergency department or your GP surgery if you have been involved in a serious incident of physical and verbal assault and one where the police have been involved

- seek support from your GP if you are on the end of persistent and habitual microaggressions in your work or any other environment and you begin to feel anxious or depressed

- stay away from substances that will heighten your anxiety or increase your symptoms of depression, such as caffeine, alcohol and drugs

- take back control in small ways (e.g. make a cup of tea, have a bath) as managing to focus and concentrate on daily activities will give you a sense of being effective in your life.

Family, friends and social networks are competent partners in your recovery process and seeking out this support is fundamental to regaining a sense of connection and getting back on track to functioning well.

When all is said and done, many BAME people find adequate coping strategies, learning to live above and beyond being the object of dislike and hatred and living for many years within a racially charged landscape – and they will continue to do so (Mearns and Cooper 2005).

Having to be 'extra good' is a refrain often identified as a common BAME experience, particularly within the work environment. Again, this is a response that has its roots in a sense that we have to do and be much more in order to earn a place within society. 'To be good, I have to be better' (Mearns and Cooper 2005, p.62).

The landscape of everyday racism, with its conscious and unconscious bias, its microaggressions, the overt and the covert, provides the backdrop. It is within this context that we need to find room and space to grow above and beyond the scene that is set and over which we have no control.

Developing resilience is a way in which we can fend off less serious mental health problems that can develop as a result of being at the receiving end of discrimination. Donald Robertson in his book *Build Your Resilience* states: 'Resilience also encompasses the notion of an ability to recover from our setbacks, coping with the consequences of adversity: buoyancy, bouncing back, recovery, getting back on your feet, return to form etc. (2012, p.4).

He goes on to suggest that we don't need superpowers to be resilient in the face of stressful situations. Generally speaking, we need qualities like confidence, and some ability to problem solve, interact well with other people and handle unpleasant emotions.

Your purpose in life is bound up in the type of person you would like to be and the ways of acting that are important to you. Values based on kindness, generosity, equality and fairness provide you with a better pathway than those centred on ourselves. As a rule, resilience that is merely bound up with individual aspirations leads to a narrow existence.

Once we have established a clearer view of our own beliefs and values, we are then in a position to move towards understanding what our purpose in life might be, regardless of the environmental impact of everyday racism.

Valuing friendship is, in fact, a constant in most people's lives and involves commitment and time, kindness, generosity of spirit, and fairness. It is not something static that requires no nurturing. To build a resilient social network, we need to be committed and prepared to sustain these fundamental aspects of wellbeing.

REFLECTION POINTS

G What is most important in your life?

G What stops you from acting in line with your values?

G What gives your life the most meaning?

G What would you live for?

○ How would you describe your values and your beliefs?

○ How might these values and beliefs guide you in making future decisions?

Form a clearer picture of the changes you would like to make – try on new behaviours, reboot and restart yourself. Make a commitment to overcoming difficulties as far as is possible while risking feeling the hurt, pain, anger and outrage, despite living through and beyond that experience of everyday racism. The more energy we invest in our personal growth, the more energy will become available. Valuing ourselves, respecting others and continuing to live with integrity, honesty, generosity, kindness and fairness will go some way in supporting new aims and objectives, new goals and purposes.

We must learn to tolerate our own complexities – balancing the good and the bad in our lives – restoring a sense of balance and meaning while continuing to be in contact with the society we live within and not cutting ourselves away from it in justifiable anger. Follow your intuition when it speaks to you of something being wrong in your life but base your responses on your values and beliefs. Be socially responsible but also individually responsible towards yourself.

REFLECTION POINTS

○ How can you exist within your environment without isolating yourself or competing with others?

○ Can you find ways to get along with others? You don't need to eliminate aspects of yourself to co-exist.

○ What shared common experiences can you find? These can become building blocks for a meaningful life with others.

There are no easy answers to difficult questions. It is tempting to create simple models that can be explained and understood in some sort of manual-like sense, but this would not reflect the complexity of the real-world cultural context in which you live.

Only you can map out your direction in life to improve and maintain your wellbeing in 21st-century Britain, creating a personal vision and discovering who you want to be and what you want from life. What will lead you to feel a sense of belonging, to feel at ease, to find a space that feels comfortable? Journeying through life with only a vague sense of direction will lead you to create 'vague feelings' and 'vague purpose'.

There are many barriers to reaching your goals, but you can begin to plan specific steps to get there and approach them with a plan of action that addresses relationships, activities, work, friendships and social life.

Learn to trust your instincts if you feel instinctively you want to be part of this group or part of that group of people because you feel less tense and more accepted – go with the messages your mind and body are receiving from the outside world. Ignore the conversation inside your head that is telling you not to trust yourself – that may very well be an old script that runs through your head over other issues. Don't be pushed too far in the direction of others' expectations and try not to rely on what makes others happy rather than yourself.

Discovering purpose in life in the area of relationships

What is your vision of the type of relationships you would like in your life, and are you able to clarify the ways you would like to connect to other people? Freedom to seek out healthy relationships where you are accepted for who you are is incredibly important, and avoiding or leaving unhealthy ones where race-based microaggressions regularly occur will increase your sense of wellbeing. Do not be forced into a space where you are constantly at the mercy of the impact of racism. Of course, we are all free to stay in relationships because we want to stay, not because we have to. Many people feel trapped in destructive relationships because they are afraid to leave, they do not trust the world beyond the hurt, and previous experience has taught them it is better to cling on to the life raft then swim to a safer shore, where they may find new friends. In order to make such a change we need to feel sure of ourselves and that we have other people to support and help us when we let go. It is much better to find some people who allow you to be uniquely who you are and not have to adapt to fit into the edges of other people's groups. Sometimes this kind of purpose in moving forward and changing your circumstances takes a lot of strength, self-control and short-term pain but staying on track and being purposeful in your search for safe spaces and inclusion is worth the hard work.

It may be that your experience of modern everyday racism as a child might make change difficult and take longer than it would for a person who has not experienced this kind of discrimination – but it is well worth working hard to alter these patterns of behaviour. Some changes cannot be accomplished in small steps; they require a leap of faith, a high level of risk, such as changing a relationship, moving to another city, leaving your job, taking up a class.

Finding purpose means restoring a sense of balance between answering your own needs and those of your environment.

Hold beliefs that give life purpose; have aims and objectives for living

- Celebrate your culture and disregard outside pressure to conform or to inform others of your perspectives – if you want to share your perspective with people you trust, then it will be safe.

- Don't measure yourself against a single standard of normal behaviour.

- Learn to be interdependent with family and community.

- Embrace new perspectives and move away from stuck and narrow thinking.

- Don't let the biases of others control who you are.

- Allow alternative approaches to aims and objectives.

Connecting with your life purpose

Each new day brings opportunities to connect to a purpose in life and provides us with a blank canvas in which to work on. We wake up and are gifted with a new day and whatever it brings us we have choices as to how we face the challenges and how we approach the good things that come our way. We can manage purpose and make meaning out of the smallest of tasks. The daily acts that come about as a result of going about the business of living, like looking after ourselves and our nearest and dearest is often sufficiently important in terms of purpose in life both on a physical and mental level. We can make an effort in these areas or we can let our relationships drift and our health and well being drift until something happens that pulls us back from the brink of an easy come easy go attitude and forces us to focus on what is the real importance of the life we have.

We can create purpose from managing our basic needs such as cooking, cleaning and caring for others and it's upon these small acts that, in my view, we build our greatest foundations; making the ordinary important. Getting this part right serves to shore us up and strengthen our ability to face the world. The human experiences is made up of the smallest of acts linked together over days, weeks and months connect us all to a deeper purpose. When faced with marginalisation and exclusion, strong foundations in other areas of life will serve to support you during times of pressure.

Much of our lives are not lived out there in a bigger better exciting world, most of our lives our lived out internally moment to moment and in the present. Your purpose in life is informed by your lived experience and the levels of race-based discrimination that have encroached upon your world and there are no simple solutions. But there are ways to work on your resilience, wellbeing and connectedness which will serve to mitigate negative experiences.

Connecting with your life purpose will be creating a wider sense of choice and a greater appreciation of your own free will and effectiveness within your world. Sometimes we cling to friends who harm us because we feel a sense of neediness – but if you have other friends, you can afford to let go and distance yourself, and if you have goals that are meaningful in your life it is also easier to let go of harmful, difficult relationships.

Key stages of the journey to achieving more purpose are described in Chris Johnstone's *Find Your Power* (2010) and can be summed up firstly by recognising that beyond our everyday lives we also experience dreams, ambitions and the desire to achieve something however modest that may be. Secondly, and on a grander scale we may feel a calling towards a destination that gets under your skin and drives you in a certain direction, moving forward and living a more expanded life.

And thirdly Johnstone advises accepting the normal levels of anxiety when trying something new, understanding that friends and family may find your change difficult to understand and accommodate, but regardless of these obstacles he suggests holding on to your goals and keeping going as best you are able.

Once you have found out what it is you would like to achieve – then it is easier to keep going when times are difficult. In his book *Authentic Happiness*, Martin Seligman describes the contribution of positive psychology which has lead to some of the concepts of wellbeing. He identifies three main approaches to improving life satisfaction and uses the terms:

A pleasant life – Increase your pleasure in small things being mindful and in the moment. Notice the beauty of the world around you and anchor some of your daily thoughts in this.

An engaged life – Develop what are called 'flow activities' – what you do to make time fly and where you are utterly absorbed in what you are doing.

A meaningful life – Add value to your world by acting for something larger than you. This can add enormous value to your life. (Seligman 2011)

The suggestion that Seligman makes is that if you want a truly fulfilling life, you need to find purpose that goes deeper than merely meeting your own needs:

We think too much about what goes wrong and not enough about what goes right in our lives. Of course, sometimes it makes sense to analyse bad events so that we can learn from them and avoid them in the future. (Seligman 2011, p.33)

Focusing on what is going well on a daily basis can be very helpful, and that might be something simple like hoovering your home or meeting up with a friend.

Meeting your own needs can leave you vulnerable, whereas caring about others puts you at an advantage because it is likely that people will return the favour and help and support you when you are in need. Relationships are fundamental to human life and as such we often need to go beyond thinking of meeting our own needs and reach out to others in order to make life meaningful and sustainable. Shared identity with a group or community leads to feelings of closeness and loyalty. It is a constant battle to find the balance between your needs and the needs of others: 'You inhabit a story that spans a wider time frame than that of your own life' (Johnstone 2010, p.256). However, we need courage to follow our own truths; we need to develop strength and resilience to experience passion, belonging and meaning when allowing our deeper purpose to act through us.

Whiteness imposes cultural domination, so that ways of thinking, family life, and patterns of wellbeing are identified as European in tradition, whereas developing a sense of wellbeing belongs to all cultures, to all peoples. Racial realities and the impact of racism need to be addressed in all areas of the current wellbeing agenda.

Charles Husband (1982) proposes three conditions which lead to a strengthening of in-group affiliations in the BAME experience:

1. *'Common identity'* (Husband 1982, p.223) – Shared experiences of racism, microaggressions and unconscious bias can lead to mutual understanding that can operate both consciously and unconsciously.

2. *'Existing groups'* (Husband 1982, p.223) – BAME staff networks or groups of friends strengthen their 'separate identity' (Husband 1982, p.223) because they may share similar lived experiences.

3. *'Existing groups'* (Husband 1982, p.223) – These may wish to include membership of white allies, or extend their dialogue to include intersectional approaches. Some members of the group may perceive that by inviting white allies they weaken their identity and subsequently seek to strengthen the group ties by rejecting outside influences.

CASE STUDY

Lewis is a 53-year-old African Caribbean man. He has strong religious beliefs and attends his local church. He is personable and popular, has a keen interest in sport and regularly organises, supports and manages the church football team, which is 80 per cent BAME men. He feels a strong sense of connection and responsibility to help those he sees struggling within his community as he fully recognises and has experienced the disadvantages and discrimination common to them all. He knows and still feels the anger towards society as a whole and as a consequence is committed to helping his team come to terms and deal with the reality of their world and his. He is also aware of the importance of the football team as it provides a means of support for the young BAME men who find it difficult to identify outside the community. He is aware of supporting their need to feel a sense of belonging and attachment as many of them regularly describe feeling a lack of ease within the wider community.

Lewis knows that his community and his church have buffered him against the 'lack of a sense of belonging' to mainstream culture and this has enabled him to feel connected with a sense of pride to his community.

In this case study, it is clear that Lewis is making conscious decisions to manage his disconnection with the majority culture through connecting deeply with his own culture. He is also connected to his church, something typically undervalued within current society but which provides him with a valuable source of connection in times of stress. He is also handing down this connection to the football team.

BAME people are visible members of a group and as such cannot disappear in society, whether they are in work or out of work, walking down the street or in a car, at school or in university; in most contexts they wear the colour of their skin.

How you are viewed by the larger group gets in the way of pursuing your purpose and meaning.

Despite the outstanding achievements of BAME people and their breaking through barriers placed unfairly in front of them, they are still regarded as less and still regarded as unacceptable.

REFLECTION POINTS

- Who am I?

- Where do I come from?

- What influences mark me?

- What have I developed for myself that is independent of the collective?

The social context you inhabit may undermine and ignore you, or react to you with indifference and anger, so if you attempt to find purpose and attempt your goals this can leave the people around you bewildered, flustered, panicked, resentful and uncomfortable.

The vast majority of the people in the world have a religious faith and even more of them maintain some element of spiritual connection and to many people. This is fundamental to their lives and certainly worthy of respect and understanding: 'No culture or society has all the answers…it is only when cultures meet on equal terms as equal partners…and express a genuine willingness to share and learn from each other (Brislin and Cushner 1997, p.151).

We can all enrich our lives through:

- kinship – co-operation

- updated experiences

- new thinking

- awareness of one's own suffering

- the value of telling your story and re-telling your story

- being aware of a bigger wider world

- maintaining a presence in every day life and living (mindfulness)

- being proud of overcoming past and hurtful experiences and dealing with the past

- welcoming the future and embracing the new you

- celebrating your own differences and uniqueness

- facing reality and developing clear and balanced views

- learning about your own culture

- co-operation and interdependence

- extended families

- respect for elders who are treated with dignity and revered for their wisdom and knowledge

- greater hospitality and expressions of kindness and support reflected through the sharing of food

- shared political histories, civil rights movements, activist movements

- a focus on commonalties that pull people together and a fostering of things that pull people together

- a focus on the building and maintaining of communities, rather than individual activities

- attending to traditional life that cares little about wealth, status, jobs or possessions

- a belief and practice of spiritual dimensions

- acceptance that race probably does matter.

When we have a conversation about racism, we are acknowledging 'difference' – the difference and uniqueness that people who are not stereotyped take as a matter of course. We all know that Christmas is celebrated uniquely in different households across the country with differing degrees of connection to Christian-based religious practices ranging from the totally secular to the Methodist, Baptist, Church of England, Catholic, Church of Wales. Not only is Christmas expressed differently along religious lines but also along the lines of different traditions. Some people open presents first thing in the morning, some after a Christmas dinner and some over the course of the day. We afford and understand nuance and complexity in UK traditions and our own practices, but we appear to stereotype other cultural and spiritual practices into straitjackets not of our own making. Complexity seems to be gifted to the majority culture.

REFLECTION POINTS

C What part does spirituality or religion play in your life?

◌ How does it support your wellbeing?

◌ What relevance did it have for you in the past?

◌ What have you lost and what have you gained?

◌ Is there anything you would like to revisit?

Mixing faith with western approaches to wellbeing is not taboo; it is as acceptable as any other thought process. Anti-religious remarks are common in our society and it is almost as if having religious views is seen as a weakness and a symptom of inferiority. I can think of many examples where we pour scorn on ourselves and others for their beliefs while failing to name, examine and analyse our own. Indeed, since we are so keen on outcomes, what are the outcomes that arise out of a secular culture?

Colin Lago (Lago in collaboration with Thomson 1996) gives an account of the Muslim Sufi approach to relieving human distress. I have simplified the steps outlined in this process.

- *Step 1* – Ensure that basic food and shelter are provided for the person in distress.

- *Step 2* – Form a contact with the 'master' (a title applicable to both genders). Allow the distressed person to talk about their problem at length and vent any hurt or pain.

- *Step 3* – Enquire into whether the person can see the conflict and resolve it.

Sufi literature and parables are there to support them – they offer a combination of nurture within a residential setting.

There have always been and always will be alternative ways of approaching well-being, effective living and maintaining good relationships. Suman Fernando calls on us to respect communities of colour and absorb the wisdom that arises out of them. We do not have to be the passive vessels of what is handed down to us from a western cultural perspective (Fernando 1991, p. 158).

White domination imposes cultural ways of being and thinking so that most patterns of wellbeing are identified as European in tradition or when appropriate are somehow seen as superior. However, most of the world is neither culturally western nor racially white; we are entitled to take on the validity of the experiences of communities of colour.

I hope this book will ignite self-discovery and inspire you to find out more about yourself and your life. You have options and choices, however limited these may be. But just as our bodies need a variety of food, our muscles need different types of exercise, and our minds need varieties of people and activities. We all need forms of connection, appreciation, companionship, security, respect and self-respect.

If we investigate our own cultures, we may be surprised to find spaces and places that can enhance our wellbeing; they are community based, and seen as having little value by the majority culture, but they have always provided us with much richness of purpose and meaning in our lives.

The importance of investigating and appreciating our own cultures and histories is summed up by James Baldwin in the aptly named *Dark Days*:

> Go back to where you started, or as far back as you can, examine all of it, travel your road again and tell the truth about it. Sing or shout or testify, or keep it to yourself: but know where you come from. (Baldwin 2018, p.38)

I am not suggesting ignoring the majority culture; we need to build an inclusive emotional intelligence, but at the same time our experience asks us to dig deep to find new answers. And these answers cannot be dealt with in simplistic terms. Rigid patterns of viewing life and living your life will only produce a narrowing down of our options and viewpoints. It seems to me that mechanistic and simplistic models, which may very well have their place as a part of the process of change towards improving wellbeing, do not provide us with the complexity that is part of all of our lives. We need to fully respond and find the means of understanding and capturing our unique struggles, our unique individuality and our connections to humanity.

The more that is taken from us through the conditions of discrimination, the more we will find sources of strength and opportunity through sheer human ingenuity. Through sheer resilience we will find ourselves more powerful and find our authentic selves.

Where to get support

- Mental Health Foundation – www.mentalhealth.org. uk/a-to-z/b/black-asian-and-minority-ethnic-bame-communities.

- Mind – www.mind.org.uk.

Appendix 1: About Legislation

In his remarkable book *The Nature of Prejudice*, Gordon Allport provides excellent arguments for the need for robust legislation, describing the ways in which different types of laws protect BAME individuals and communities that 'equalise advantages and lessen discrimination' (Allport 1954, p.461). Having the mechanisms to check overt signs of prejudice creates a public conscience and raises a standard of expected behaviour.

The whys and wherefores of the Equality Act 2010

This book is primarily about wellbeing, about finding a sense of belonging and inclusion. For this reason, we only touch upon the most recent legislation. In the words of Binna Kandola:

> Whilst the legislation is very important, it is clear that it is not going to bring about the positive changes that were intended... Fundamentally, diversity is about behaviours and outcomes. It's about how relationships are enacted. It's about how we perform in everyday situations, based on how we think – and how we think about how we think. In other words, diversity is a process, not a structure. (Kandola 2009, p.19)

Nevertheless, the current anti-discrimination legislation does provide us with a framework in which to promote change and protect the rights of individuals against discrimination, and it is essential to social justice and change within our society.

Most of us will now be familiar with the nine protected characteristics covered by the 2010 Equality Act:

- age

- disability

- gender reassignment

- marriage or civil partnership (in employment only)

- pregnancy and maternity

- race

- religion or belief

- sex

- sexual orientation

Citizens Advice has produced an informative yet easy-to-read document that explains how the Act protects people from discrimination (available at www.citizensadvice.org.uk/law-and-courts/discrimination/about-discrimination/equality-act-2010-discrimination-and-your-rights).

Appendix 2: Useful Terminology

It is useful to explore the following definitions:

- Race

- Racism

- Unconscious bias

- Prejudice

- One drop rule

- Colourism

- Discrimination

- Microaggressions

Race

According to Charles Husband (1986, p.206), 'Race, is a classification based on the belief that the perceived difference is immutable and fixed… Although the concept of a "race" has no scientific backing its salience as a social category is evident throughout British Society.'

It is commonly accepted that Race is a 'social construct' and affects the world in which we live politically, socially and economically. It impacts on our everyday lives but has no scientific worth, value or substance.

However, race has a meaning, and for the purposes of this book we will be looking at 'race' mainly in terms of personal identity. Sewell (2009, p.14) notes: 'The biological basis for the division of humans into races is flawed... The genetic differences within so-called racial groups are sometimes greater than those between people of different races.'

Racism

In addition to more official definitions of racism, the first three explanations of the word 'racism' provide more of a 'feeling tone' to the descriptions:

> To be black was to confront, and to be forced to alter, a condition forged in history. To be white was to be forced to digest a delusion called white supremacy. (Baldwin 2018, p.5)

> It is racism that is the active principle. Racism is then essentially about institutionally generated inequality based on concepts of racial difference. (Fernando 1991, pp. 24)

> Discrimination comes about only when we deny to individuals or groups of people equality of treatment which they may wish. (Fernando 1991, p.52)

> "A belief that human races have distinctive characteristics that determine their respective cultures" usually involving the idea that one's own race is superior and has the right to rule other." (Katz 1978, p.51)

> Racism can be understood as an inability to accept and acknowledge differences of race. It might involve the treatment of some people as inferior because they belong to a particular race, and it is usually used to demonstrate disapproval. Where racism is present, there is an attempt to control and dominate the object that is felt to be different and separate. (Bhui 2002, p.130)

Lastly and so powerfully put in its simplicity:

> I do not always feel coloured. I feel most coloured when I am thrown against a sharp white background. (Rankine 2014, p.52)

Unconscious bias

A briefing by The Royal Society provides the following definition: 'Unconscious bias is when we make judgements or decisions on the basis of our prior experience, our own personal deep-seated thought patterns, assumptions or interpretations, and we are not aware we are doing it' (Royal Society 2015).

If a part of our mind in inaccessible to us, we may behave automatically and without thinking. This is perfectly normal and has always been a means by which humans have survived. Making unconscious decisions is a part of our everyday lives – we don't need to re-learn how to ride a bike or turn on the washing machine – these actions have become automatic. In a sense we automatically have a positive bias towards:

- positive bias towards our in-group
- negative bias towards an out-group.

There is a tendency in all of us to stick to our own kind of people – to people who are like us. But there are people out there who do not fit in with our 'in-group' and we have a tendency as a society to label these people as part of the 'out-group'. It is of course natural to spend time with people 'like us' and unconscious bias is something we all have in common.

However, this bias produces faulty thinking because it relies on over-generalisations, narrow focus and misattributions.

Prejudice

Allport provides us with a simple and yet powerful description of the term prejudice: 'Whenever a negative attitude toward persons is sustained by a spurious overgeneralization, we encounter the syndrome of prejudice.' (Allport 1979, p.12) And Kandola adds: Prejudice, however, does not even have to be something of which we are conscious. For example, we may not be aware we are categorising people (Kandola 2009, p.54).

Modern life involves screening and sifting through a constant stream of information needed to make sense of the world around us, and responding with speed. We are neurologically programmed to make very quick decisions that can be based upon perceptions that may be faulty and can lead us to be prejudiced.

One drop rule

Whilst there have been efforts to expand categories, we are still left with the legacy that anything other than white is sub grouped. And the notion that one drop of black blood originating from your ancestral heritage will categorize you as black and not white even if your skin colour is white! Such is the power of the non-scientific term race!

Colourism

Colourism refers to discrimination based on skin colour. Typically it disadvantages dark-skinned people, and privileges those with lighter skin (Okereke 2013).

Discrimination

Discrimination is a mechanism by which you are treated unfairly and unequally because of your race. For a more in-depth understanding of discrimination the equality and human rights commission provide us with a definition of 'discrimination' and this can be found at https://www.equalityhumanrights.com/en/advice-and-guidance/what-discrimination.

Microaggressions

Derald Wing Sue provides a comprehensive explanation of the term 'microaggressions':

> Microaggressions are the everyday verbal, nonverbal, and environmental slights, snubs, or insults, whether intentional or unintentional, which communicate hostile, derogatory, or negative messages to target persons based solely upon their marginalized group membership. In many cases, these hidden messages may invalidate the group identity or experiential reality of target persons, demean them on a personal or group level, communicate they are lesser human beings, suggest they do not belong with the majority group, threaten and intimidate, or relegate them to inferior status and treatment. (Sue 2010)

References

Adegoke, Y. and Uviebinené, E. (2018) *Slay In Your Lane*. London: 4th Estate. An imprint of HarperCollins Publishers.

Akbar, A. (13 January 2010) 'The many faces behind the veil.' *The Independent*. Available at: www.independent.co.uk/news/uk/this-britain/the-many-faces-behind-the-veil-1865772.html.

Alleyne A. (2004) *Race and Culture. The internal oppressor and black identity wounding*. Available at: http://aileenalleyne.com/wp-content/uploads/sites/6/2013/06/internal_oppressor_black_identity_wounding.pdf

Allport, W.G. (1954) *The Nature of Prejudice*. Cambridge, MA: Perseus Publishing.

Angelis, T (2009) Unmasking racial micro aggressions. American Psychological Association. Available at: www.apa.org/monitor/2009/02/microaggression

Angelou, M. (2014) *Rainbow in the Cloud. The Wit and Wisdom of Maya Angelou*. London: Virago Press.

Baldwin, J. (2018) *Dark Days*. London: Penguin.

Baumgarte, R. (2016) 'Conceptualizing cultural variations in close relationships.' *Online Readings in Psychology and Culture*, 5(4). Available at https://doi.org/10.9707/2307-0919.1137.

Bhugra, D. and Bhui, K. (2001) *Cross-Cultural Psychiatry: A Practical Guide*. London: Arnold Publishers.

Bhui, K. (2002) *Racism and Mental Health: Prejudice and Suffering*. London: Jessica Kingsley Publishers.

Brislin, R.W. and Cushner, K. (1997) *Improving Intercultural Interactions: Modules for Cross-Cultural Training Programs Volume 2*. London: Sage Publications.

Brislin, R.W. and Suzan Jane, S. (1997) 'Power in the Service of Leadership.' In R.W. Brislin and K. Cushner *Improving Intercultural Interactions: Modules for Cross-Cultural Training Programs Volume 2.* London: Sage Publications.

Butler, D. (2018) 'Opinion. Race. If Alan Sugar can't see why his Senegal 'joke' is racist, then sack him.' *The Guardian.* Available at https://www.theguardian.com/commentisfree/2018/jun/21/alan-sugar-senegal-joke-racist-sack-bbc-tweet

Burton, K. and Platts, N.B. (2006) *Building Self-Confidence for Dummies.* Chichester: John Wiley & Sons.

Byrd, A.D. and Tharps, L.L. (2001) *Hair Story: Untangling the Roots of Black Hair in America.* New York, NY: Saint Martin's Press.

Cabinet Office (2017) *Race Disparity Audit. Summary Findings from the Ethnicity Facts and Figures Website.* October 2017 (Revised March 2018) Crown Copyright. London: Cabinet Office.

Carlson, R. (2008) *Don't Sweat the Small Stuff...and It's All Small Stuff.* London: Hodder & Stoughton.

The Civil Service. (2014) 'Ethnic Dimension. Research and Consultancy. Identifying and Removing Barriers to Talented BAME Staff Progression in the Civil Service.' *Qualitative Research Findings.*

Cousins, S. (2010) 'Isolation in the workplace.' *Counselling at Work* (now *BACP Workplace*), Issue 70, 13.

Cousins, S. (2011) 'Self-care for black and minority ethnic practitioners.' *Healthcare Counselling and Psychotherapy Journal* 11 (4): 12–15.

Dienstbier, R.A. (1989) 'Arousal and physiological toughness: Implications for mental and physical health.' *Psychological Review,* 96 (1): 84.

Diller, J.V. (2007) *Cultural Diversity. A Primer for the Human Services.* Belmont, CA: Thomson Brooks/Cole.

Eddo-Lodge, R. (2017) *Why I'm No Longer Talking to White People about Race.* London: Bloomsbury Publishing.

Eleftheriadou, Z. (1994) *Gateways to Counselling Transcultural Counselling.* London: Central Book Publishing.

Equality and Human Rights Commission. (2016) *Healing a divided Britain: the need for a comprehensive race equality strategy.*

Fanon, F. (1961) *The Wretched of the Earth.* London: Penguin Books.

Fernando, S. (1991) *Mental Health, Race & Culture.* Basingstoke: Palgrave MacMillan.

Franklin-Boyd, N. (1989) *Black Families Therapy. A Multisystem Approach*. New York, NY: Guilford Press.

Garcia, H. and Miralles, F. (2017) *Ikigai: The Japanese Secret to a Long and Happy Life* (Trans. H. Cleary). London: Hutchinson.

Gibbs, G. (1988) *Learning by Doing*. Oxford: Oxford Brookes University.

Hall, S. (2017) *The Fateful Triangle; Race, Ethnicity, Nation*. Cambridge, MA: Harvard University Press.

Her Majesty's Inspectorate of Constabulary and Fire and Rescue Services (2018) *Understanding the Difference: The Initial Police Response to Hate Crime*. Available at: www.justiceinspectorates.gov.uk/hmicfrs/wp-content/uploads/understanding-the-difference-the-initial-police-response-to-hate-crime.pdf.

Hirsch, A. (2018) *Brit(ish): On Race, Identity and Belonging*. London: Jonathan Cape.

Husband, C. (1982) *'Race' in Britain. Continuity and Change*. London: Hutchinson & Co.

Iyer, D. S. (2013) Six Ways To Help Your Child Cope With Racism – Part 2. Psychology Today. Available at: www.psychologytoday.com/gb/blog/life-liberty-and-the-pursuit-insight/201311/six-ways-help-your-child-cope-racism-part-2

Johnstone, C. (2010) *Find Your Own Power. A Toolkit for Resilience and Positive Change*. East Meon, Hants: Permanent Publications.

Kandola, B. (2009) *The Value of Difference. Eliminating Bias in Organisations*. Oxford: Pearn Kandola Publishing.

Kelley, N., Khan, O. and Sharrock, S. (2017) *Racial Prejudice in Britain Today*. London: NatCen Social Research.

Kelly, J. (2007) 'Rise in hate crime in England and Wales.' BBC News. Available at: www.bbc.co.uk/news/uk-41648865.

Khaleeli, H. (28 October 2012) 'The hair trade's dirty secret.' *The Guardian*. Available at: www.theguardian.com/lifeandstyle/2012/oct/28/hair-extension-global-trade-secrets.

Lago, C. and Barbara, S. (2003) *Anti-Discriminatory Practice in Counselling & Psychotherapy*. London: Sage Publications.

Lago, C. (in collaboration with Thomson, J.) (1996) *Race Culture and Counselling*. Buckingham: Open University Press.

Lawton, G. (26 August 2017) 'Living on the borderline: How I embraced my mixed-race status after years of denial.' *The Guardian*. Available at: www.theguardian.com/lifeandstyle/2017/aug/26/living-on-the-borderline-how-i-embraced-my-mixed-race-status-after-years-of-denial.

Lindenfield, G. and Vandenburg, M. (2000) *Positive Under Pressure*. London: Thorsons.

Littlewood, R. and Lipsedge, M. (1982) *Aliens and Alienists. Ethnic Minorities and Psychiatry*. London: Penguin Books.

Lue, L. (2003) *Nonviolent Communication Companion Workbook. A Practical Guide for Individual Group, or Classroom Study*. Encinitas, CA: Puddle Dancer Press.

Mearns, D. and Cooper M. (2005) *Working at Relational Depth in Counselling and Psychotherapy*. London: Sage Publications.

Neff, K. and Germer, C. (2018) *The Mindful Self-Compassion Workbook: A Proven Way to Accept Yourself, Build Inner Strength and Thrive*. New York, NY: Guilford Press.

Palmer, S. (2002) *Multicultural Counselling. A Reader*. London: Sage Publications.

Rankine, C. (2014) *Citizen: An American Lyric*. Minneapolis, MN: Graywolf Press.

Reid, S. (13 August 2018) 'How to deal with microaggressions as a black woman.' *The Guardian*. Available at: www.theguardian.com/lifeandstyle/2018/aug/13/sharmadean-reid-bossing-it-micro-aggressions.

Robertson, D. (2012) *Build Your Resilience. How to Survive and Thrive in Any Situation*. London: Hodder Education.

Ryde, J. (2009) *Being White in the Helping Professions*. London. Jessica Kingsley Publishing.

Ryff, C.D. (1989) 'Multidimensional model of psychological well-being.' *Journal of Personality and Social Psychology*, 57(6): 1069–1081.

Sandhu, R. (17 May 2018) 'Should BAME be ditched as a term for black, Asian and minority ethnic people?' BBC News. Available at: www.bbc.co.uk/news/uk-politics-43831279.

Seligman, M. (2011) *Flourish: A New Understanding of Happiness and Well-Being – and How to Achieve Them*. London: Nicholas Brealey Publishing.

Sewell, H. (2009) *Working with Ethnicity, Race and Culture in Mental Health: A Handbook for Practitioners*. London: Jessica Kingsley Publishers.

Shukla, N. (2016) *The Good Immigrant*. London: Unbound.

Sue, D.W. (17 November 2010) *Microaggression: More than just race*. Available at: www.psychologytoday.com/us/blog/microaggressions-in-everyday-life/201011/microaggressions-more-just-race

Suler, J. (1996, revised 2007) 'Online therapy and support groups.' *The Psychology of Cyberspace.* Available at: http://users.rider.edu/~suler/psycyber/therapygroup.html.

Sullivan, J.M. and Cross Jr., W.E. (2016) *Meaning-Making, Internalized Racism, and African American Identity.* New York, NY: University of New York Press.

Sunderland, M. (Illustrated by Armstrong N.) (2008) *Draw on Your Relationships.* London. Speechmark Publishing Ltd.

Turner, C. (27 December 2017) 'Prince Harry interviews Barack Obama on Radio 4: Ex-President warns social media is corroding civil discourse.' *The Telegraph.* Available at: www.telegraph.co.uk/news/2017/12/27/prince-harry-interviewsbarack-obama-radio-4-ex-presidentwarns.

UNESCO (United Nations Educational, Cultural and Scientific Organization) (2009) *UNESCO World Report: Investing in Cultural Diversity and Intercultural Dialogue.* Paris: UNESCO Publishing.

Van Deurzen-Smith, E. (1988) *Existential Counselling in Practice.* London: Sage Publications.

Vernon, M. (2013) *Use Philosophy to Be Happier.* London: Hodder and Stoughton.

Versi, M. (27 June 2016) 'Brexit has given voice to racism – and too many are complicit.' *The Guardian.* Available at: www.theguardian.com/commentisfree/2016/jun/27/brexit-racism-eu-referendum-racist-incidents-politicians-media.

Walker, A. (1982) 'Embracing the dark and the light.' *Essence*, pp.67 and 128 (reprinted from Black Scholar, March–April 1973).

Wijeyesinghe, C.L. and Jackson 111. W.B. (2001) *New Perspectives on Racial Identity Development. Integrating Emerging Frameworks.* New York, NY: New York University Press.

Wooley, S. (2018) 'The role of higher education in reducing disparities in race.' *Chair of the Government's Race Disparity Advisory Group, Director of Operation Black Vote. HERAG Think Tank 5.*

X, Malcolm and Haley, A. (1965) *The Autobiography of Malcolm X.* New York, NY: Grove Press.

Zehr, H. (2002) *The Little Book of Restorative Justice.* PA,United States: Good Books.

Index